FROM THE WISHMORE TO YOU

FROM THE WISHMORE TO YOU

RUTH ANNE
AND JANICE ABEL

FROM THE WISHMORE TO YOU

*Sisters Growing Up
in the '40s*

PUBLISHED BY ABEL PUBLISHING
BOX 1034
CEDAR FALLS, IOWA 50613

Library of Congress Catalog Card Number: 98-92729
ISBN: 0-9655739-1-5 (PBK)
ISBN: 0-9655739-2-3 (HDBK)

FOR OUR PARENTS

If we could just collect and wrap in little gifts,
Each kind of memory joyful in our life,
We'd have a whole holiday set of presents,
To open in the Golden December of our life.

One wrapped from each one in our family.
One for the love-filled fun together.
One wrapped for joys of nature.
One for each milestone we managed to weather.

Each one filled with little charms
that flashes back a thought.
A thought that brings back all the love
once given and cheerfully brought.

So- - -just drop a charm into a little box
for memory's sake alone.
Wrap it carefully and beautifully and
keep it in your heart's home.

Then someday when life is bleak,
and all the world seems gray.
Open up your
"Now which gift shall I open today?"

AUTUMN, 1976

Dear Reader,

If one picture is worth a thousand words, there must be a lot of words in this little book. We had no idea this project would become a book. As we were going through treasures of the past, the pieces of our childhood came together through pictures and other memorabilia. We started to bring together pictures found in Dad's meticulously filed negatives and photos. The photos would trigger a thought of times past, and as we talked we realized we each experienced some of the same times very differently. Because of our current lifestyles, we began writing letters to one another. Reminiscing helped us travel through a journey that has led us to a better understanding of ourselves and each other.

Our childhood is unique to us, but it is a reflection of the times. You can probably see yourself and your friends in many of these situations, especially if you grew up in a small town in the Midwest in the '40s—this could be your life. We have visited with many people in the writing of this book. When we talk of the times past, a certain sparkle comes to the eye, a knowing laugh, and an "oh-yeah" comes bursting out with the memories that we recall.

We hope that our stories will prompt you to talk to others, your grandparents, your parents, and other family members about your own childhood. You have within you information and stories that you have forgotten that you know! Everyone should do a writing of their childhood and growing up—wherever it may be. The following generations will thank you for writing, and you will enjoy reliving some of the past through your memories.

To encourage you to record some of your memories, we have provided prompts along the way to encourage you to recall and write about your life. So get out a pencil and paper and have it handy as you read our stories. Our "Wishmore" for you is that you will make this a personalized beginning for telling your childhood story.

Writing about growing up in Iowa adds understanding to the diversity of world culture. We hope these stories will touch those of you from other cultures and places to help you better understand and appreciate our heritage.

We are living proof that it takes a village to raise children. Our parents were masters of family values, yet we were influenced and guided by all those around us. We were street kids who were loved and watched closely by the Main Street "family."

This is your invitation to step back to the '40s in the small town of La Porte City, Iowa, and join us in our journey through these pages of time.

Regards,

Janice and Ruth Anne

OUR STORY IS ABOUT...

How many times can you find Faye? What was her schooling? Locate Faye's watch and bracelet (lower left) given to her for high school graduation. Find picture of brother Glen twice. Find Faye with sister Nina. High School graduation picture(upper right), Faye seated third left. Look into her eyes, and feel her smile.

With every galloping charge, Faye's short legs bounced on the sleek bare back of the giant horse beneath her. Tightly grabbing the flying mane, she prayed she would make the next bend of the river road, and above all, not be thrown off at the bridge. Faye loved horses— especially this one, Big Byrd, 12 years of age, as she was, too. After a sauntering spring morning ride to her uncle's neighboring farm, they were going home. Fast! Big Byrd couldn't be stopped. Faye wrapped her arms around the stretching neck and buried her face in the mane. Hearing the sound of hoofs on the old board bridge and then off on the other side, she gave a slight sigh, but to her great surprise Byrd made a quick turn for a shortcut home. Through ditches of wild rose thickets, the scent of roses whisk through the air. Then, with a bounding vault to green meadows, the mare stretched for home.

Faye caught the thundering rhythm of the flying force beneath her. Now mounted jockey like, slightly rocking forward on bent knees, Faye took command. Next the orchard. Dash left, duck, steady, move right, and around. Sa—lap! Through spring snows of floating apple blossoms they flew. Into the barnyard, Big Byrd charged, rearing wildly! But only once. Faye making a confident jerk on the reins, they made a final grand circle. With the halt, the spirited giant abruptly became the serene mother she was. Her colt jauntily threw his head up to greet her. Big Byrd nudged him gently. Lathered, pink petals laced her mane and hung to her skin. Faye sat back, gave a sigh, and catching her Dad's image in the corner her eye, smiled wishfully.

"So, Faye, looks like you have had a run for the roses and won today!"

This is our mother, born with the spirit, and grace of this captured moment. She was the middle child of John and Olive Sheffler Burrows. She grew up on a farm with her younger brother Glen and older sister Nina.

The generations before us.
Faye Abel, Olive Burrows,
Janice Abel, Emma Sheffler.

Find George's bead work (convalescent time). Find George on horse and in band. Find sister Florence with George. Locate picture of his dad riding horse on brick main street.

Arm stretched out pointing upward to the ball on top of the La Porte water tower, George said boastingly, "I stood on that ball!" The truth was he did—but before the tower went up! George had a knack for finding devilment in activities. It was also reported that one morning a citizen, one of few sporting a brand new Model T Ford, found his car parked on top of the bank! George and some of his friends worked all night, taking the car apart and putting it back together again in this new lofty location!

This is our father, the oldest child of Ed and Kathryn Hunter Abel. He grew up with his younger sister, Florence, in the town of Mt. Auburn, Iowa, and they later moved to La Porte City when his father became the city Marshall.

At an early teen age, George wanted to join the Navy, but his parents would not give him permission, and the school basketball team insisted that he stay with them. The following year, 1920, while playing basketball during his sophomore year, he had an unfortunate accident and was unable to finish school or participate in any more sports.

The local newspaper reported:

"The boys game was called off in the second half on account of the Center Point refusing to finish. The treatment given the La Porte City team was anything but on the square and the action of the Center Point team and those who had the game in charge is said by those in attendance to have been disgraceful and unbecoming high school pupils."(*Progress Review*, February 19, 1920)

The game that followed was also reported.

"Misfortune has landed doubly hard on the boys basketball team and just when they had the easy end of the season before them. The Shellsburg team played a good game and won from us by a score of 21 to 15. The La Porte City team was seriously crippled by the loss of two regulars, Weldon Betts and George Abel. Weldon was ill and though George made a game effort to play the first half of the game he was unable to do much because of the injury received in the knock down drag out affair presented to us by the Center Point school the previous Tuesday."(*Progress Review*, February 26, 1920)

As a result of basketball injuries, George developed osteomyelitis. In these days before miracle drugs such as penicillin, fighting such a disease involved surgeries and for George many long months in Iowa City hospitals. George was left permanently with a stiff right arm and with a disease that infected bones in a chronic way over many years.

George was not one, however, to be easily defeated. He used his time of recuperation to think about options. While keeping his hands busy with crafts and projects, and his mind busy learning the Morse code, he started to make a plan for his place in the world. Having been out of the public eye for som etime, he needed something that would help him to regain his confidence and build for his future. The beginning of his plan would be the opening of a popcorn stand in La Porte City.

Though Faye and George knew one another's names for some time, as would be true growing up in any small town, the spark of romance between them did not happen until some years later. Faye had just graduated from Gates Business School and was working on a fund raising campaign for Allen Hospital in Waterloo. It was a typical Saturday night, summer, 1928. The crowds were mingling in little groups all up and down the main street of La Porte City. Faye had come home for the weekend and planned to meet her sister, Nina, in town on the hotel corner. Bustling through the crowd, they finally found each other. "There you are!" Nina said with a smile and a sisterly hug. "We'll have time to shop the shops and maybe get in the early show before Harry gets off work. How has work been this week?"

Faye sighing replied, "Just fine. The fund drive for the new addition is going great, but each donation causes the paperwork to get deeper and deeper." They slowly moved down the street to take in the windows of the shops. "Looks like everyone is doing well here in La Porte City. I always like the hometown stuff. How's Mama and Papa?"

"They are busy with the field work, but they should be in sometime tonight. Pop always likes to stand on the corner and get the news—even if he is tired. Let's stop for some popcorn—it won't spoil our dinner if we eat late. I'm famished!"

Glancing up from his work, George looked directly into the brown eyes of a beautiful young girl he had known by name only for a long time. Seeing her now with a smile and a twinkle in her eye, he noticed a special something he had not seen before. There she was, the love of his life, and it just took a special moment like this to realize it. "You look like two hard working girls. Have some popcorn on me." From that evening on, his mind was filled with Faye Burrows. He had business plans buzzing around in his head, but he wanted to share his life with someone very special, and he knew she was the one. Faye, too, had the glow of love in her heart even though her father, John, didn't think too kindly of the romance at the time.

"How can anyone make a living selling popcorn?" her father John exclaimed. "Too much a schemer. Besides, his dad packs a gun! He has no future. He's not a farmer!"

Nevertheless, George and Faye were married on May 5, 1932, in the home of Clinton Smith, minister and superintendent of Allen Hospital. They honeymooned at a cabin at Clear Lake, and their lifetime partnership had begun.

Notes about your father, mother, and family. Where can you get more information?
Who should you talk to?

YOUNG PEOPLE
ARE WEDDED

George F. Abel and Miss
Faye Burrows are Con-
tracting Parties.

A wedding of considerable interest in the younger set is that of Miss Faye V. Burrows and George F. Abel, both of this place, who responded to the marriage vows last Thursday afternoon, May 5th. The service was read at three o'clock by Rev. Clinton F. Smith in his home in Waterloo. The bride wore a becoming gown of pink chiffon and had a corsage bouquet of roses and sweet peas. After the ceremony lunch was served by Mrs. Smith.

The bride is the second daughter of Mr. and Mrs. John B. Burrows, who live west of town, and is a prepossessing young woman. She attended the La Porte City high school, completing the course with the class of 1926. Later she was graduated from a commercial school in Waterloo. For the past three years she has held the position of secretary to Rev. C. F. Smith, who is superintendent of Allen Memorial hospital in Waterloo, and will continue in that work. The groom is the only son of Marshal and Mrs. E. H. Abel and has always lived in this community. He attended the public school but, owing to poor health, was not permitted to complete the prescribed course. For the past year he has been the proprietor of a sandwich shop and refreshment stand on Main street, and the couple will make their home here.

They have been receiving congratulations and best wishes from their numerous friends for their future happiness and prosperity.

Locate lace handkerchief carried at Wedding! Look closely, what did the wedding announcement call Faye?!

What was the price of a hamburger? Look at free merchant gifts. What did the Wishmore offer? Find Pastime Theater picture. Find Faye twice(seated far left in street scene). Find the radio! What a great afternoon to listen to a baseball game!

Yes, in reply to George's father-in-law, papa John Burrows, the beginnings of George's business all started with popcorn, but it didn't end that way! Returning to La Porte City after many months over a period of several years in the hospital, George never returned to school. George's uncle and friends helped him build a popcorn house, and, with permission from the city, he located it on the corner of Main and Chestnut Street next to the Briardale store. George already had a charming personality and gift of gab, a sharp business head, and support from his family and friends. All he needed was a little time and luck to get the thing going. For the next few years, George and his mother worked the steam-driven popcorn and peanut machine. He made a profit and began developing the idea of a food business that the town of LaPorte City could certainly use. He knew he had to start small, pay as he went, and keep his overhead low.

Not only was his business outgrowing the little popcorn stand, but the automobile traffic was increasing to the point it was no longer feasible to have the stand on the street. Needing a change of location and a way to expand business, George relocated the stand at lots 207 and 209 West Main and announced his opening of the Wishmore Sandwich Stand on October 16, 1931. Why Wishmore? Originally, the name Wishmore came from a brand of spices bought from a dealer to mix in with hamburger for a sandwich. Over the years, "Wishmore" took on greater meaning and became a '30s and '40s icon for the cafe on Main "with all wishes and more" for its daily customers.

George had picked an opportune time to open the Wishmore. The very next month the Pastime Theater reopened after being "wired for sound" for the new talking pictures. Located directly across the street from the Wishmore, night life in LaPorte soon centered on attending a movie and either before or after having a sandwich at the Wishmore. "Bank night" at the theater became a favorite community activity. Theater owner, Marvin Fosse, and local merchants offered a drawing of cash and merchandise each week. If your number was drawn, you could win! The amount started at $15 and, if not claimed, it would carry over to the next week, and the amount would grow. A big winner might go home with $100! The theater also had a Popeye club, in which a wooden Popeye doll was given away to children.

The little Wishmore became a hub on Main for town chatter and eating. A window allowed George to serve to the outdoors on Main Street. You might call it the beginning of fast food, complete with a pick-up lane. Customers walked by the window to pick up their sandwiches. The cover photo and photo (page 18) illustrate the appearance of the Wishmore in 1931 and 1932. The small interior had only the 4 stools, but there were places to sit outside on the sidewalk! George provided a bench, and someone had even brought rocking chairs to sit on!

The attraction to the Wishmore was not only the food but also the radio that George had mounted on a shelf. Many radio broadcasts were of interest—national news, presidential speeches, baseball games, and prize fights. Later, when the counter inside was enlarged, the radio was moved indoors as the indoor photo illustrates (page 23). Notice also in this photo the restaurant license, the prices of some of the foods, and some of the items on the counter. As we were researching for this book, we enjoyed looking at the details of old photos with a magnifying glass. We recovered details lost in the far corners of our minds.

It was also indeed fortunate for the little Wishmore that the very next fall (1932) the first Jiggs Day was celebrated. It was the largest one-day celebration in Iowa. Jiggs and Maggie, a comic strip favorite, were featured in the parade. Corned beef and cabbage, a Jiggs favorite, was served free. The *Progress Review* reported that more than 5000 people visited town on this day. For days following the celebration, chatter around the Wishmore declared Jiggs Day a great success.

"George, your Wishmores are great, but that corned beef and cabbage feed was the best."

"We never had, in my 31 years experience, a better, cleaner, celebration," C.A. Brust, grocery proprietor, declared.

"We've got to do it again!" Dr. Paige exclaimed.

"It showed that we are more than just a small town!" Dr. Bailey announced. "Plans are underway to make this Jiggs Day an annual event." Even though the city appointed a committee of citizens to oversee the next year's event, many ideas jelled around talk at the Wishmore.

The "Wishmore Cafe" became a truly family affair. George did most of the work himself, used his own ideas for most all aspects, and relied on family help. By this time, Faye had come into the picture. She, too, had a good business sense and a wonderful country background of cooking and baking. She was willing to work and to make it a family concern.

The little building was bulging. Although summer offered seating on the sidewalk, additional seating was needed during the winter. During the late '30s, the counter was expanded to seat 12, and an addition with five booths was also completed. This made it possible for families or larger groups to gather for an evening of activities.

The menu soon expanded beyond the successful Wishmore sandwich that cost 5 cents and was served any time of day. George and Faye offered 25 cent lunches, homemade pie for 10 cents, and a full steak dinner for 35 cents. Mr. Percy Haven would bring a chunk of ice early each morning to cool the pop for the day. Soon Mr. Potter of Potter Ice Cream from Waterloo offered to set in an electric ice cream machine, and ice cream was made available in La Porte!

With the highway going past the cafe, George decided it was important to keep the shop open 24 hours. The night traffic, mostly trucks, would certainly help build a reputation for good food any time of day. Before long Faye and her sister Nina were baking pies and making Wishmores as fast as they could to keep up with the local trade and the added demand from the highway. Help beyond the family was hired to keep up with the growing demands.

On any given day, tuning into the chatter around the Wishmore counter gave you a sense of life in LaPorte—not always the quiet tranquil community and not always gossip. But opinions were always given freely!

"So, did you hear about Doc Paige getting robbed last night?"

"No, how did it happen?"

"It all happened when he and his daughter, Marie Jean, came home last night. He rents Nell Gannon's garage, back close to Big Creek. It's pretty dark back there. Doc tossed his wallet at him, and he fled with it. Mary Jean said she hid her purse under her coat. Anyway,

Doc lost about $20 dollars!"

"That robber knew what he was doing. Doc's are the only ones around here with that kind of cash. Last week it was Doc Fields. Any clues?

"None yet, far as I know."

"Say, did any of you read the piece that our editor, Everett, wrote last week for the *Progress Review*, stating we were all pretty much on our way to another world war? I hope he's not right about that. Let's stay out of the Europe mess! We've got too many good things going on right here!" Heads nod in agreement, an unusual occurrence around the counter.

"Talk about getting things going. What do you think of Glen's newly renovated store?"

"Not been in there yet, but that new front sure looks fancy. Someone was saying it's just like store fronts found in big cities. The black glass front reflects like a mirror. You can see sky reflections, and in late afternoon I bet I could stand across the street and shave myself! The little wife was in there yesterday and got me some handkerchiefs for only 5 cents, and she also got herself a pair of silk stockings for 25 cents. We're thinking about a fan, too, only $1.00. It really is a variety store now. Glen told me the sign would be across the whole front and read '5 & 10 Byam's Variety Store—$1 and up'."

"Glen is really looking forward to the summer band concerts that will bring business to town. In fact, have you heard that Karl King is going to be a guest conductor for one of the concerts in June?"

"Who's Karl King?"

"Why, Jake, that's Karl King, the well-known Iowa composer. I bet every band in the country plays Karl King marches. You know, the one we hear all the time, Barnum and Bailey's? He started out with the circus. He's from Fort Dodge. It's a concert not to miss. I'll bet there will be almost as many people in town that night as there are at Jiggs Day."

For the most part life in a small town during this time was relaxed, routine and very predictable. On occasion, however, there was the unpredictable, and one such time was on a Monday morning early in April, 1940. The day started out as usual, at the Wishmore. The locals were gathered around the counter hashing over Saturday night's events. They suddenly heard on the street chanting sounds, "We want Goff. We want Olson." Students holding banners were marching down Main. The band led the group. It seemed the whole school body was parading! Not very much ever moved the counter locals too fast, but on this day everyone jumped up and pressed their faces to the window. "What are those kids doing out of school? There's young Rampton with them; he was in here this morning delivering milk and didn't say a word about anything like this."

About that time, the door swung open, and Everett Smith, the *Progress* editor, entered in a flurry, breathless. He gasp, "The whole high school student body walked out of class this morning."

"What's this all about?" one asked.

"If you asked me, they should be all kicked out of school," another declared.

"Well, it seems," Everett continued, "you know, we need a basketball coach. Well, Taylor simply can't do superintendent work and coach, too. So, in that Goff and Olson are the only male teachers to do it, the board temporarily held up their contracts until a choice could be made between the two."

"What's with the school board anyway?" another retorted. "Couldn't they think of a better way to resolve the problem than hold up the contracts of two well-liked teachers?"

The students gained a following. As they passed by the Wishmore, with the exception of one or two, customers joined the parade back to the school. By noon, the students returned to school. Art Olson became the coach, and both men received their contracts. The afternoon buzz at the Wishmore was full of pronouncements about what was done, or should have been done, long before the *Waterloo Courier* and the *Progress* printed it as a headline!

No one knew at the time how the little Wishmore would continue to grow and become central to community activities. With a counter for 12 and five booths, customers were served well until the years following World War II when the dining room was added. With this, the Wishmore provided for an even wider variety of community activities.

Over the years the cafe went through a series of name changes, beginning with Wishmore, later the GFA Cafe, and last on the marquee, simply Abel's Cafe. Regardless of the name on the marquee, the name Wishmore always stuck best! There was something about it. Maybe a bit of magic in Wishmore? Perhaps, but probably, more simply, it became a place where people gathered to take a break from the chores of their day. Regardless, together George and Faye fashioned the place for their work, for their family, and for their community.

Notes about how your family made their living. How did work life come about?
How did family and work go together?

Note Corned Beef and Cabbage given free — Jiggs Day. Mayor's office.
Find George twice. Find the radio!

LETTERS TO MY SISTER

To understand the references in our letters we would like you to know about our family. Ruth Anne has three grown children, Randall, Cynthia, and Ronald. Grandchildren are Nick, Jake, Sarah, and Jason. Ruth lives on Terrace Drive in Waterloo, Iowa. Her two cats, Tigie and Priscilla keep her company. Janice lives on Rownd Street in Cedar Falls, Iowa, and shares a home with Mary Lou Hunt. They have an 8 lb. Yorkie, named Toby, and puppy Tasha! Enjoy our letters and remember to start writing some of your own.

Find Ruth's first birthday cake. How many dolls can you find?

DECEMBER

Dear Ruth,

I don't know about you, but I really had a great time going through some of Mom and Dad's pictures the other day. The one of Mother looking directly into the camera is a real treasure, and the one of Dad in a suit, I believe is one that was in his school annual. I was curious why Dad wasn't in the basketball picture, so I called Aunt Florence, and she told me that the picture was taken in the Spring after basketball season. Dad probably would have been in the hospital at that time, since he was hurt in the first part of the year, 1919.

Mom's jewelry is a charm. I know she especially cherished the bracelet given to her at graduation. You wore her wrist watch for a while when you were in high school, right? And Dad's bead work! It is such fine work; I have a hard time imagining Dad having the patience to do it.

At any rate, Ruth, I had so much fun recalling some of our childhood; I wonder if you would be interested in making a concerted effort to recall some earlier times on a regular basis. It could be primarily through letters since we don't see one another too often. I know you are busy teaching, but you are good at organizing your time, so writing letters seems like a good idea. Letters would also be good to share with others.

I will talk with you about this when you come to our New Year's Party. Mary Lou and I have been making plans for New Year's Eve. We will stay home. Of course, we will be celebrating your Birthday as well. What a deal to be able to celebrate a birthday on New Year's Eve! Don't bring anything; I'll have the birthday cake and the New Year's balloons!

Until I see you New Year's Eve,
Your sis, Janice

JANUARY

Dear Janice,

Another New Year has begun—the time seems to go faster every year. Thanks again for helping to celebrate my New Year's Eve birthday with fun, and good cheer. You have a way to help everyone have a good time. You always come through with a surprise or two. Do you remember the story our parents used to tell us about New Year's Eve? The baby (new year) would come chasing the old man (old year) through the house at midnight. We were never able to stay awake to see if it were really true.

The birthday cake you baked was perfect, and the candles remind me of the warmth and love I feel each time we spend a special day together.

I am always happy to see you—your conversation gives me comfort.

I've enclosed several pictures that I found of us together. Just *look* at us in these pictures!

There we are together like gifts to each other, heading toward a lifetime of opportunities. Your expressions vary from joy to frustration to shared wonder of the world. I think this is a nice collection of pictures. I am sure we can make a collage of them and still see the necessary details. Things like your guiding hands in the sandbox, your big bow in the hair, playing dolls, cowboys, winter fun, and the backyard tent. I even spy Nancy Gae, our Cedar Rapids cousin, guiding us and loving us as always. She was just enough older that I'm sure we looked up to her much as I to you.

You look as if you would like to give the crying baby comfort or something! And there you are covering your eyes so you won't see the wobbly 1 year old poking around on the birthday cake. Weren't those two pictures taken in the livingroom of the house on Locust street?

This reminds me that Mom finally did get her new home. Wasn't that a wise and carefully planned decision? And just in time for my arrival the last day of 1938. It wasn't long, though, that more space was needed. In later years Mom told me that she didn't have room for the high chair in the narrow kitchen, so two more rooms were added.

Mother did everything she could to keep our family in a normal routine. It would have been easier to bring food home from the cafe or have everyone go there to eat, but instead she would make dinner at home so we could sit around the table together. I especially recall Mother standing at the stove making fried potatoes, using a tin can to chop them as she cooked. Still today, the smell of fried potatoes takes me back to 604 Locust and the comfort of home.

Wasn't Mother a good time manager? She worked, planned, and still had time to spend important moments with us. She carried on with a sweet smile. She was the rock of the family. Now with Mother gone—it makes even more sense to have a sister. You and I are the extension of her, and now we need each other more than ever. Looking at these pictures reminds me of how much I loved my childhood. We did have a happy childhood, didn't we?

Growing up, it seems to me, we had some of the typical sister arguments. It seems most often our arguments centered around sharing space. After we graduated from baby beds, we slept on a studio couch bed. I remember, you would draw an imaginary line making a crease in the sheet. "This is my side, and this is yours—stay on your own side of the bed!" I don't think we ever had knock down, drag out, hair pulling fights. On the other hand, we rarely had the joy of a quiet tea party with our dolls. I remember admiring your doll more than mine and wanting it, but I was glad you had it, too—I thought you should have the best. Seems like we were always carting our dolls around—wrapped in blankets, in the doll carriage, in the wagon, on the sleds. We had bikes, swings, and a backyard tent. We played cars and trucks in the sandpile. I watched you play with trains and erector sets. I imagine you watched me play with tinker toys, Lincoln logs, and dolls. I still have a set of cardboard farm animals that we played with a lot.

Didn't we love playing outside? Any season of the year we could be found out in the yard doing something. I liked to run around the house shooting our toy guns. Your big hair bow didn't quite fit with the cowboy outfit, but you always wore it. Playing cowboys was one of the lasting pastimes of our childhood—maybe because we saw a lot of cowboy movies. The days of arguing about Roy Rogers and Gene Autry passed away much too quickly— or have they passed? We always had something fun planned. Just as you often do today.

You and I were buddies; I needed you.

As we grew older, there was a time when our play interests didn't coincide, but that seemed to be all right, no big deal. I had my friends; you had yours. Now again, it seems natural that our bonds have grown stronger as we have grown older together.

You mentioned Mom's jewelry—it *is* a charm. I have enjoyed wearing some of the treasured pieces. Her class ring fits on my pinky, just as it was made for her hand. Yes, I did wear her watch when I was younger. It was adjusted very small to fit my wrist. I hope you don't mind, but I took the liberty of framing one piece of Dad's bead work, the initial "A," to keep it safe and secure.

Just as you are there with me in those pictures, beside me, watching me, guiding me, you are here today. You have always watched me with careful anticipation—you've been there to help when you can, share the joys and sorrows of our family events, give advice and words of wisdom. Your smile has always been there to pull us through. I have discovered that of the many photographs of you—almost all are smiling—or a look of deep thought—both of which you are good at doing! I could not have asked for a better sister—you are the best!

It *is* a good idea to write letters to each other about our childhood. It is a great way to come together and share our lives again—it's almost like being a kid again.

I hope your coming year is prosperous and pleasant—that we will share some special times together again soon.

Oh—Sister!! Ruth Anne

Write about special times with your brothers and sisters. Talk to them.
Jot down ideas. If details do not come easily,
come back to your notes later.

FEBRUARY

Dear Ruth,

Thanks for all those pictures you sent. The picture of the two of us (center) with you holding the doll was a captured moment. I remember when this picture was taken at a Waterloo studio in the downtown Black's Department Store. Mom rushed out to buy you something so you would be more cooperative. You got the doll, and I didn't! So much for being good!

Ruth, looking at the pictures of us, especially the ones of winter, I am reminded of snow pants. When I was in first grade, Mother told me to be sure to put on my snow pants even when I went to recess. It took me so long to get them on, I would miss recess! Sometimes I felt like Mom and Dad restricted me too much; regardless, I did what they told me even if I was the only one to miss recess!

You mentioned building the house and moving to Locust Street. Obviously, you don't remember; you weren't born yet. But I spent my toddler years at home on Main. Mom and Dad lived with Dad's parents, Ed and Kathyrn. We lived in the building on Main next to the cafe. It was handy for us with the folks just starting a business. Grandmother took care of me often so that Mother could work at the cafe. I found many pictures of the family and me in the back yard as well as on Main during this time.

Here is one of my favorites: Mother holding me. It was taken at the back door of our Main Street home. I like it so much because I think it captures a glimpse of Mother's strength just by her presence.

Yes, Ruth, I am sure that Mother yearned for a place of her own, and that's why they bought the property on Locust. In the meantime, all was not roses with Grandpa and Grandma, and, for reasons unknown to me, Grandpa moved out before our parents moved to their new home. This left Grandma Abel to move with us. I was never aware of how Mother felt about this, but I can imagine she had mixed feelings.

I was about 3 when Mom, Dad, Grandma Abel, and I moved "home" on Locust. I found the bill of sale for the home property at 604 Locust that shows Dad bought the property from Gertrude Gardner in February of 1936. Remember Gertrude? She lived next door to us for years. The first summer the folks had the lot, they planted tomatoes for use at the cafe.

You mentioned being told of the need to add to the house when Mom didn't have enough room in our narrow kitchen to set your high chair. That all prompted the first change to the original house. Thinking about it, Ruth, there were a total of six changes to the original house including the addition of the garage and then renovation of the garage to Dad's TV repair shop! Each addition was predicated, I am sure, not only on needing the space but also on having the money. Next time I see you we can talk about this. Also, Ruth, with all this talk about house changes, I especially recall the story about Dad changing the heating system. I will write about it and hopefully get it enclosed with this letter.

Our home served many purposes over the years as the needs changed. Do you remember our victory garden? Dad has movie pictures of us in the garden. The other day I was talking to Mary Lou about our garden and its similarity to a victory garden, and she didn't know what a "victory garden" was! While a victory garden might look similar to vegetable gardens we have today, the food these gardens yielded represented a significant part of the food needs of our country during the war. Many foods were rationed, so to stretch the use of coupons many Americans planted gardens. According to the Reader's Digest publication, *Our Glorious Century*, July 1996, about 40% of the nation's vegetable needs were provided by victory gardens in 1943. Also, a victory garden was a concrete way to show that you were contributing to the war effort. Patriotism was at an all time high!

Another effort the folks made to produce food during the war was one you probably don't remember. Dad had a chicken house built on the property. The chicken house sat where the garage now stands. I recall several things about chickens. Dad does have an 8mm home movie of the chicken house being built. I hope to find it and send it to you. The chickens were great to have on hand, but it was quite an ordeal when it was time to kill and dress them.

Because we did have chickens, my first pet was a rooster I named "Jerry." It all started when as a little chicken the other chicks would not let him close to the food, so I would chase them away. Well, Jerry grew up to be a handsome rooster. He roamed freely around the neighborhood. He would hide in the raspberry bushes where I do believe he knew the sharp thorns on the bushes would stick me, when I went to pull him out. I had him long after the chicken house was gone.

We only raised chickens for two or three years, and then Dad sold the chicken house. The image of the chicken house being moved off the property is clearly etched in my mind. A crew put it on skids and pulled it across Gertrude's garden plot. This was, of course, after the fall harvest. It was a hot day, and all that remained was the smell of the chickens and burning autumn leaves.

Ruth, between the two of us, we have memorabilia and pictures that reveal a lot about our home life. Dad, you, and I on bikes in front of the house shows the first addition of a dinette and also Dad's radio room. The three of us rode bikes often; Mom never did. Dad's humor is reflected in the picture of the two of you. Notice your hat; it is a May basket turned upside down! Also, the center picture of us was taken on an Easter Sunday. But

NION
White
Lisbon
Bunching
VICTORY
GARDENERS'
GUIDE
WALT DISNEY'S
MICKEY MOUSE

Just a spot to call our own. We'll find per-fect
LET THE REST OF THE WORLD GO BY
BALLAD
Priscilla and John Alden

more than that, on this picture, when I enlarged it, I could actually see far in the background, the swing suspended from the two oak trees that stand at the Sides' residence! I spent many hours on this swing with Bev and Shirley Sides. You did, too, remember?

Of all the memorabilia we have, a favorite of mine is the little plaque of Priscilla and John Alden that was given to the folks when they were married. Through the years it hung in so many places in our home. You may not know this, but one day Mom asked me what I might want after she died. Without hesitation, I pointed to the little plaque. You have probably spied it already hanging in my study, and I am sure it will be there for as long as I am on this earth!

Note the original, tattered sheet music of Mom and Dad's favorite song. You probably would agree, Ruth, that the family did not gather around the piano often to sing, but once in a while we did. Mother loved music, and it was her interest that brought us the piano. She would play several of her favorites from the Golden Book of Songs. Most often, she would play a song whose words were: "We'll build a sweet little nest somewhere in the West and let the rest of the world go by." That was the only time Dad would sing along. It was their song and their dream that they made come true.

I especially like the picture of us in front of the house that shows our small play car parked on the right side of the porch. The peddles gave it power! Now, I need to get my power going over to Waldens Photo for prints of some of the pictures we took last week.

Till I see you next,

Love, Janice

I didn't realize it at the time, but we were very fortunate to have conveniences that others did not have. We always had central heating in the house, but I recall that for many years our grandparents had a heat stove in every room. I distinctly remember when we had a furnace and stoker that burned coal. Each year, Dad had coal shoveled through a basement window into a makeshift coal bin. Because I was small enough to fit between the top of the coal pile and the ceiling rafters, he had me crawl to the window in the coal room and lock it to keep mice and other possible intruders out. I recall it so vividly. Dad would lift me up into the full room of coal, and I would have to be careful not to hit my head. I would place papers ahead of myself so as not to get too dirty. The fresh coal was extremely black and oily. I liked to do it because I was doing something no one else could do! Another part of all this that impressed me was taking the burnt coal, the clinkers, out of the furnace. During the winter, we would stack them all around the furnace in pails. Dad used them on the drive when the old Ford got stuck in the snow or ice.

The days of forced heat using coal, however, were short-lived at our house. Dad always wanted to stay on the leading edge of things, and so he had installed a radiant heat system in the house. This heating system used hot water traveling through copper pipes with fins running under the floor. He designed the system so that we would have even and efficient heat. He placed a thermostat in every room to control temperature. In order to monitor the circulation of hot water usage, he had a set of clocks, one for each room, located next to the boiler room indicating how much time each room called for heat. In order to determine the difference in temperature from floor to ceiling, he had thermometers hung close to the floor and some near the ceiling in nearly every room of the house. One of the disadvantages of radiant heat, in contrast to forced air, is that it takes a longer time to bring the temperature to a desired level. To compensate for this, Dad made a box housing a thermostat and attached it to the outside of the house. To me it looked like a simple wooden box, but it worked! When the temperature outside fell sharply, the boiler was called on to begin heating water, thus anticipating the change in temperature.

Life with Dad left us always expecting changes of some sort. I looked forward to the conversation these changes generated. I recall St. Clair, from the plumbing and heating company, shaking his head and saying, "I don't ask why; I just do it." Yet I know he was very curious about what the result would be. In this case, we grew up with warm floors and a home free of drafts. To this day, I have a difficult time in the winter with my cold floors!

Dear Jan,

The snow this morning reminds me again of winter days growing up in La Porte City. I do remember the clinkers and getting them out of the furnace with a special grabber with a long handle. The clinkers "clinked," the coals glowed, and the heat blazed on our faces. Do you remember getting dressed in front of the heating register in the living room? Grandma Abel helped us get dressed because Mom was at work. We listened intently to Uncle Stan and Cowboy Ken on a WHO radio program that challenged us to get dressed faster. It was a race between the boys and the girls. The host of the show would ask you to raise your hand when you were dressed. "Looks like the girls won today," he would say. It worked—we were dressed in no time. We could sure use something like that for today's kids.

I was so happy living on Locust, and wasn't it great that everything was so handy? We lived only two blocks from the cafe and Main and just one block from the school. We both started with first grade at the school on Commercial Street. No kindergarten or pre-school then. I'm sad this school no longer exists, but the old must make way for the new as time goes on. I feel sure that the apartment building now located on that property serves a very important purpose to the community.

Before I was old enough to go to school, I always looked forward to you coming home from school. You would come racing in the door. I suppose you were hungry like most kids are after school. You would dish up ice cream. I would have some, too, and always a cookie. As you recall, Janice, this scene is captured in our home movie "Just Another Day," along with many other scenes of our daily routine. I ran the film just last night, and there we are around the red trimmed dinette table. We must have been packing valentine cookies for school, and I'm eating them as you and Mom are packing them.

Wouldn't you agree that much of our life revolved around that red trimmed table? There was always laughter. Mom and Dad would start laughing about something simple, a situation or a circumstance. Sometimes, even though I couldn't see why they were laughing, I would soon find myself laughing, too.

Besides everything else that happened at this table, I especially recall the weekly "check-up" for the business at the Cafe. I can still see Mom and Dad sitting at the dinette table counting the money in a wooden cigar box. Dad divided the cigar boxes into compartments to accommodate coin sizes. Bills for the week were placed on a wooden spindle. Mother entered figures on a ledger. It was quite simple in the early days. They paid the bills and put anything left in their pocket.

Wasn't Mom a talented person? She could do so many things. She was a very good cook. Not only did she enjoy trying new recipes and collecting some of the best but also making up her own to perfection. In her later years she made "Thumbprint" cookies that everybody in the family likes. I share these with others often because they look like little bird nests. My children always have liked Grandma's thumb prints. I've enclosed the recipe, in case you get the urge to make cookies this Valentine's Day and can't find your copy. (hint-hint)

It was always amazing to me how Mom had a knack for creating a pretty corner in so many places—at home, in the backyard of the cafe, in the dining room, on any table where she served food. Remember when she had the carpenter build in a corner desk in the living room? If you can't recall it, drop over and see it in my basement. It is serving as a storage shelf here on Terrace Drive. There were other built-ins, such as the corner cupboards in the dinette for her candlewick glassware. Treasures like these are hard to come by. You know I have them now, but if you ever want to use them, just let me know.

Mom added many pretty touches to our home. I remember seeing the Workbasket magazine at her fingertips. With those talented hands, she not only cooked and baked but completed some fine needlework. I don't know how she found time to crochet. Somehow she just made time, for it was a relaxing, enjoyable hobby. She tried many kinds of handiwork, but crocheting was probably her favorite. The crewel butterfly pictures she said were "cruel." I tried teaching her how to knit, but she always went back to crocheting. Among my many treasures of the past are some of the handworks that Mother loved doing. I hold dear the cat faces that she embroidered for me when we were making dozens of little stuffed cats. Because of her, we had white doilies for the end tables and embroidered pillow cases and dish towels. Picture stitcheries decorated the walls, and in later years she made afghans of all colors. And there were always flowers. Mom loved flowers. So many of her furnishings had blossoms—carpeting, chairs, curtains—it was virtually a '40s flower garden.

I have a wonderful afghan with roses that she made. Do you still have the 1976 American flag afghan she made for you? I have mine. Wasn't she the patriotic one?

In the evenings our home was filled with sounds from the radio. I especially liked The Green Hornet, Fibber McGee and Molly with the famous cluttered closet, and Sky King. Blondie and Dagwood could always make us laugh. I remember how thrilled I was to see the first Blondie and Dagwood movie to finally see the people we'd heard so many times. We always had to send for the newest Sky King ring and could hardly wait for it to come in the mail. One was a glow-in-the-dark ring; one had a magnifying glass on it. One had a secret compartment, another a ball point pen. I've searched for the Sky King rings but can't seem to find any. Do you have any?

Now there are some wonderful copies of the Fibber McGee and Molly radio programs on tapes. I hope you have time to listen to them soon, as they will certainly take you back to the '40s into the living room at 604 Locust. As we were there, listening to Fibber McGee, we waited with great anticipation for him to open his closet. It was fun to hear all the things fall out—usually in about the same order. It is hard to imagine that this was just sound effects and not the real thing. Radio personalities had a wonderful talent in painting pictures with sound. When Tonto stopped his horse quickly to join his partner, "The Lone Ranger," I could almost feel and smell the dust from the road. We spent many evenings listening to radio shows.

Playing 78 rpm records and coloring pictures was on the top of my list of things to do back in the '40s. I had an Army uniform and a toy rifle. I used to play "You're in the Army Now, You're Not Behind the Plow" on the record player. I'd march around and around the house from room to room.

Remember reading comic books and the little fat books about cowboys, etc.? Later, I became interested in the Nancy Drew mystery books. Did you ever read any of these? But wouldn't you agree, over the years, that having a doll or train to play with was always one

View of Locust street. Center, porch of the Sides Home.
Far right, Gertrude Gardener home. See map, page 101.

Our Home, 604, Locust street. See map, page 101.

Janice, Nancy Gae Goon, cousin; and Ruth.

of our favorite pastimes?

Another important part of our home was having a pet. You took to the animals much easier than I. I was always a bit frightened. I believe we started out with a stray dog—you know, that one with the wagging tail and the friendly face that just wanted to be loved? We named him "Tippy." I really don't know how long we had him or what happened to him, do you? But he was the start of the pets in our home. Next we had a Pomeranian named Mitzie. She scared me because she was so quick and yippy. I always climbed on the sofa to get away from her. I remember leaning over the edge and petting her for the first time—and how proud I was to have done that. After that, I was her friend forever. Mom and Dad both liked animals and always supported our interest in them. Remember when Mom and Dad took care of your little Yorkie when you returned to graduate school? And always, Dad would pick up the camera and catch a snapshot of the family pet. No wonder we continue to have them in our lives today.

You probably remember that my children had a dog named "Pud," and now it isn't surprising that they as young adults have pets, too. My own long interest in cats came back from the days of my childhood.

Thanks for taking care of my cats when I go to visit Cindy, Nick, and Jake in Texas. Priscilla and Tigie are wonderful lap cats and appreciate your loving attention. If you bring Toby along, it gives them something to perk up their day.

Better close for now. Tomorrow is a school day, and I have lots of snow to go through, so I'll have to get up early. These winter days remind me of times my daughter and I went sledding. I am sending you my poem that says how I felt.

See you soon,

Ruth Anne

Gertrude Gardener, Faye and Ruth.

"Let's go sledding," I heard one day.
  As I was scrubbing the floors.
"Just look at the snow and the drifts on the hill.
  Let's go sledding in the bright outdoors!"
I looked at the snow,
then the floors,
        then her face.
        Then a smile came over mine.
        The floor can wait,
        The snow will melt,
        And someday I'll miss that girl of mine.

                "Let's go," I said, as I dumped the pail.
                        And quickly tidied the room.
                "Let's find our boots, our mittens and scarves.
                  We'll have time for a fun afternoon."
                        She giggled a giggle of anticipation.
                                And I, too, giggled inside.
                        You'll never know how close you can grow
                                On a cold winter, wonderful ride.
The snow crunched under our boots,
        The runners eased over the snow.
We boarded the old sled, braced our feet,
And hung on tight. — "Ready to go?"
" Ya, I guess," she said with a giggle.
" So am I, Here we go!"

                        A big push started us down,
                                The cold air rushed at our faces.
                        The wind whistled through our scarves,
                                Seems we were off to the races!

I hope we'll never forget the
        seeing, feeling, hearing
    Of that winter day on the hill.
    The sparkle of the day,
            The sting of the ride,
            The slash of the runners,
            The excited giggle inside.
                Forget? — We never will.

                We rode many times that day.
                Trying to make each ride a bit longer.
                Each ride more thrilling some way.
                We knew we would soon have to stop,
                But each trip down was well worth
    The long pull back to the top.

The afternoon went by so very fast.
    We knew something so wonderful couldn't last.
        But then—we didn't miss it,
            Have it we always will,
        Just close your eyes, smile, dream a while
                And we'll be back on the hill!

WINTER, 1975

Christmas 1943 at 604 Locust. Note lower right snap. Spy John Alden plaque hanging in far corner.

To: Ruth—Have I ever told you about my favorite Christmas?
From: Janice

Ruth, you talk about trains, dolls, and snow—Christmas was the time they came to us! Somehow Mother and Dad were able to capture the magic of Christmas for us, better than the ones found in storybooks! One Christmas that was extra special to me was the year Santa brought us an electric train, not a wind up one, mounted on a 4 by 8 plywood base. There was a village that included a railroad station, water tower, and an army of marching soldiers.

Aunt Florence, Uncle Bill, and cousin Nancy Gae spent Christmas with us that year. I am sending you pictures of this Christmas. You can see your little face just above the table. You can see Nancy Gae and me in the picture, and I know at the time we must have been thinking about the train. We knew if we didn't get done eating and to the train, Uncle Bill and George would beat us to it. Later Dad and Mom talked about the difficulty they had getting the train up from the basement to the living room and under the tree. They had to take the train out the back door, wade through the snow, and take it in the front door. What a time Santa Claus had that year, but they laughed about it for years. I believe they had as much fun at Christmas as we did!

Now every year, even though I have the merriment of family and friends at Christmas, I try to find "Christmas" but never quite do. You asked me why this is true. I really don't know.

Yes, Christmas and other holidays were important to the family, but don't you think Dad's hobbies brought a much richer and different dimension to our everyday living? Dad's amateur radio interest even brought on a special language. Remember all that "ham talk"? An "XYL" was a wife of a ham operator. We are the daughters of WØKLC; we are called "yl's." That means, "young lady." This YL is signing off until I see you next. I hear my sweet little Yorkie yipping. She wants out!

See you,

Janice

P.S. I can't find a Sky King ring. Probably best left to a memory anyway.

Dear Jan,

Thanks for the letter recalling your Christmas memories. Christmas is a magic time for everyone from young to old. It makes kids of all of us, doesn't it? You've not lost your knack for enjoying the wonderment of the holiday. It is just that you're looking at it from a different perspective. Continue to enjoy it as if you were a child.

I liked the bubble lights and the smell of the real pine tree. You may know, there is now a modern version of bubble lights. I must investigate them for the next holiday season. That surely will bring back the childlike wonder of Christmas for me. I still feel the delight in my heart when on any Christmas morning I see a new doll. I can smell the newness of the clothes and touch and feel the newness of the doll's eyes and hair. Remember the dolls with the lamb skin hair? They had flirting eyes that would move in all directions. I sent you pictures of them in one of my earlier letters.

As is probably true today, some of the best moments of Christmas came from the anticipation. I recall getting out the nativity set, carefully unpacking each piece, and placing the characters here and there. Changing them around and enacting the story was a favorite way to pass the time until Christmas Eve. Then I liked lying under the tree and looking up through the lighted branches as we listened to Christmas music, waiting for the big event. When are you going to get out that old nativity set and use it again? I know you have it.

Looking at the pictures of Christmas, obviously we were always blessed with many gifts. There we are by the tree in the living room. If you look closely, or use a magnifying glass, you can see the corner desk and there above it is the plaque of John and Priscilla Alden! I sure like seeing the evidence of our past in the things we found and have here in the present. Treasures to behold!

I'm anxious to hear from you again. Do tell me more about the ham radio stuff. I don't remember much—just a little about Dad rushing home from the cafe to answer the "Iowa Net" at noon.

Signing off for now,

Ruth Anne

Notes about home and family traditions. Describe where you lived. Important holidays. Make a list of important objects from your childhood.

Decode the morse code message. W . _ _ I . . S . . . H . . . . M _ _ O _ _ _ R . _ . E . F . . _ . Y _ . _ _ U . . _ Find George with best ham friend, Pete. Details of QSL card. Microphone and key.

Dear Ruth,

"CQ, CQ,CQ—This is WØKLC, King, Love, Charlie, calling. 'CQ,' how about a contact? Are you there, Pete?" These words reverberate in my head. After closing the Cafe and coming home, Dad would get on the "rig" and "ham" it up. I was awakened many nights hearing him in the next room calling, "CQ." I would listen to the conversations and the laughter late into the night.

Dad designed and printed his own QSL card. These cards were used to verify contacts ham radio operators made with one another. Dad had cards tacked all over his radio room. It was a collection of a sort. When Dad first became a "ham" operator in the late '30s, his call letters were W9KLC. There were some changes in the amateur operators numbering system, and in later years, the nine on Dad's call letters became a zero. Look on the QSL card I have sent you. There are several things designated on it. One is the type of transmitter. Dad's was a BC 610 as is indicated on the card. I could never forget it. It was a huge transmitter that sat on the floor in his radio room. Dad had the floor reinforced to handle the weight. He did not allow us near it. He said the magnetic waves would not be good for us! Anyway, we believed him at the time! His QSL card also shows the horizontal antenna he had suspended between 2 forty-foot towers placed on opposite corners of our property. Pictures of the family were often taken next to these towers. Notice the photo of Dad by the tower. This picture is one of my favorites. Many people came to see these towers as they were the highest ones in town with the exception of the city water tower!

Of all the hobbies Dad had over the years, don't you think ham radio was the most enduring? I know that Dad became an amateur operator in the late '30s and that he had to pass some kind of a test to get a license. Part of it involved knowing how to use Morse code. Dad called it "keying." I never remember him using the key too much. I imagine it was a transition time from key to voice, but I do remember him practicing to read and send code. Once, I became interested in it and sometimes would copy it. I didn't do it by writing the letters, only by writing the dits and das, and then Dad would translate it, telling me where I missed.

One summer I went with Dad and Pete (WØOJD)—you know, his best ham friend—to a radio operator picnic in Marshalltown. They rigged up a horizontal antenna for the car, using two cane fish poles anchored to the front and back bumpers. They carried the transmitter in the trunk and could only operate it from the trunk. The more modern type becoming available, mobile units installed in cars, were shown at this gathering. Needless to say, Dad and Pete had a different style, and this drew a lot of attention!

What the world wide web and the internet are doing for us today, the ham radio did for Dad in his day. Ruth, he made contacts and had friends from all over the world. I know he especially liked 75 meters because he would talk to operators in the Midwest and have on-going contacts. He operated on other meters, but "they didn't seem to be as dependable," as he put it. Some nights the "skip" was different, the cloud cover and all, and it would be more difficult to make the contacts he wanted. This is all recollection on my part, of course, but I vividly remember the conversations he carried on over the radio waves. I don't know the circumstance, but I do know that one time Dad handled messages for soldiers on a ship, so they could communicate with their families.

Wasn't ham radio a good niche for Dad? He loved to talk to people. It was an identification for him, and over the years he made many friends. Ruth, remember one of our first family trips was to a ham friend in Muskegon, Michigan? We visited Hal and his wife Rae, and the vacation was filled with picnics and gatherings with other radio operators. Dad looked forward to times when he could "eye ball" a ham he had only talked to on his rig. More than likely anytime a stranger would knock on the door it was a radio operator that Dad had not seen before. Their voice would give them away, and they were welcomed into our home as if we had always known them.

I am not sure when Dad added radio and TV repair to his agenda, but it was not only an extension of his radio knowledge but really helped with family finances.

Now I realize photography must have been high on Dad's lists of interests. Having recently spent considerable time in the darkroom printing some of his black and white photographs, I am beginning to realize the breadth and diversity of the kinds of pictures he took. My plans are now to bring together Dad's history in the photography world. I think I can piece it together looking at the different kinds of pictures he took at different times.

73's for now; that means signing off.

Love, Janice

*Notes about family hobbies. Recall a family event surrounding a hobby
or meeting of other families or friends. Can you hear what your mother or
dad might have said?*

Find wind-up movie camera. What did they feed that dog? Ruth in action; Ruth's Easter bonnet. Ruth's reflection in the black table top!

Dear Ruth,

I traced Dad's photography career through the cameras he had. In the earliest days, it must have been a box camera. Most of the pictures of the '30s and some '40s were snapshots. The negatives are sharp and enlarge fairly well. The earliest 8mm movies date back to when you were a few months old. Let's see, 1939! I would estimate the earliest movies of Main Street are from about that same time. The 8mm camera with the windup key is a gem. And it still works!

The Rolleicord with a square negative took most of the black and white photos during the '40s. I know Dad had a press camera that used film packs he would change with each exposure. This he used during the mid-'40s primarily for taking inside portrait-type pictures. It was during this time that Dad built the darkroom in the basement. Later in the '40s he took colored slides from the Rolleicord. When the 3-D slide camera became available, he had one of those. The 35 mm Minolta snapped the last of his pictures.

I admired Dad's great passion for everything he did. I believe that is one of the great things I learned from him. Pursue with passion! Dad would talk to everyone that knew anything about what his interests were, and he would read everything he could find on a subject. Photography was no exception. At any given moment we could expect Dad to ask us to have our picture taken, usually for a specific purpose. He might be curious about a specific camera setting or angle to get a particular effect. I thought he was trying to catch me at my most unattractive times. In my awkward adolescence, I imagine it would have been difficult to catch me otherwise. I would complain, "Wait until my hair looks better, or I have on something different." He would reply, "That's o.k. I just want to see how this new film will work."

Consequently, Ruth, have you noticed how ridiculous we look in some of these pictures? I don't want anyone to see pictures of me in some of the outfits I wore. Flowered shorts and stripped shirts! And my hair, wow! It looks like I hadn't combed it for a week! I have sent you a few that aren't so bad. Of course, they are of you! Ha! Look at the picture of you jumping rope. I am sure Dad wanted to catch the rope mid-air and not be blurred. Also, the picture of you sitting at the black table. Here, I am sure he wanted to capture your reflection. That was but another of his many photo experiments.

When Dad started a project, I could always count on being his "go-for" for this or that. As I recall, you never were too involved in these projects; perhaps you were too young. I would always get curious myself. He would have parts strewn all over the floor and often would write out plans on bits of paper, nothing fancy. Remember when Dad constructed an electronic flash? This was when flash bulbs and flood lights were common. Having read about possibilities of an electronic flash that could be used repeatedly, with the same bulb and would recharge itself, Dad didn't rest until he had a flash apparatus completed. It was a large intruding piece. He built it on a wooden pop case. Capacitors were part of it. They look like square cans lining the box attached with a tangle of wires. Some way he charged it up. He used a screwdriver to discharge it when he was finished. With its look of something from a different planet and the cracking sound of the flash, we never had to be told to stay away from it. But it worked, and he had a flash unlike any other local photographer.

For me, the darkroom was the most exciting. You were there part of the time, I remember. Dad partitioned off the front part of the basement under the living room. He had plumbing completed to have both hot and cold water to control the temperature of chemicals. He installed appropriate lights. I looked forward to working with Dad when he printed pictures. As we slipped the exposed paper into the developing solution and tipped the pans to and fro, the images would begin to appear as though they were coming from another time or world.

Dad was meticulous in tracking the process and printing for different effects. He would burn in parts of a negative to get a balance of exposure, or fade in other parts. I am sending you a copy of a dog picture that he made for our Valentine. It is about the only special effect I could find of his work.

There, of course, is the famous picture of us riding an oversized dog. Dad carried a billfold size of it in his wallet. Customers, some strangers, would actually ask to see this picture. What was then quite a curiosity would be commonplace today.

I hadn't been back in a darkroom until the past year when I made contact prints of Dad's negatives. The first time, returning to the darkroom with its distinctive odors and lighting, it seemed like once again I was standing beside Dad, only this time I didn't have his guiding hand.

Will talk with you soon about photos you have found.

Jan

Notes about family pictures. Where to look?
Who can you ask? Better yet, keep good pictures here on!
Find a favorite family picture and describe it or events surrounding
the picture in as much detail as possible.

To: Ruth—Hope you enjoy this as much as I did writing it.
From: Janice

Reviewing the horse racing events one early day in 1962, Faye discovered that the Kentucky Derby would be running on the very day of their 30th wedding anniversary.

"Isn't this a sign or something? How could we not go?" she related to George. He made no reply. "I can send for tickets; the address is right here in the paper," she confirmed, cajoling him a bit more.

"So?" George replied, but he knew better. He might as well give in. "Well, o.k.," he softly replied, hoping she wouldn't hear. Faye didn't miss his mumbling and promptly sent for the tickets.

For Mom this meant a lifetime dream coming true; for Dad, it meant doing one of the things he dreaded most, going into a city. Faye's anticipation of the trip grew over the months. She planned every detail. She made herself a new print flowered dress. She bought George a white shirt and a pair of dark blue pants with matching suspenders, and she brushed up his best straw hat, one with a little feather in the band. When it was time for the trip, Faye packed two big suitcases, a styrofoam cooler filled with sandwiches, and a thermos of hot coffee. The night before the Derby in a motel north of Louisville, George pored over maps planning every turn, and a back-up route in the event any turn was missed, while Faye studied once again every bit of information she had been able to find about the horses running in the Derby.

Before the crack of dawn the next morning, they were on the road. Without a flaw in George's road plan, they arrived in the parking lot of Churchill Downs at 7:30 a.m. No question, they were one of the first spectators to arrive for the 88th running of the Kentucky Derby May 5, 1962! They sat in the car sipping hot coffee until the doors opened.

The weather was as perfect as their day would be. The southern sun and the smell of spring flowers filled the air. They found their seats, and Faye began scanning the program of races, one by one. The Derby run would be the 7th race of the afternoon.

"Who do you like for the big race?" George asked, looking for advice.

"The favorites, Ridan and Sir Ribot, both look o.k., but..." replied Faye, pausing and looking over her notes, "so far as I am concerned, it will be number 3, the dapple gray."

Overhearing Faye's remark, a well-dressed gentleman sitting nearby quickly interjected, "Grays don't win the Derby." Looking at Faye and tipping his hat a bit, "Little Lady, take my advice. Willie Shoemaker on Sunrise County is a much better bet!" Faye and George soon made their bets, on number 3, the gray; Bill Hartack would be the jockey.

Faye finally heard a call from the stands that she had long been waiting to hear, "Get your mint juleps here. Ice Cold just $1.25!" Faye promptly waved her hand. She certainly didn't want to miss one of the great Derby traditions. A slender figure carrying a wide rack of iced glasses caught her signal and made his way to their seats. "How many would you like, ma'am?" asked the ruddy-faced little guy.

"I don't care for one myself," George said politely.

"Yes, you do want one," Faye cut in.

A bit surprised, George replied meekly, "Oh, o.k.," and took the one Faye had shoved toward him! Both sat quietly, sipping their drinks, savoring each sip, not only of the drink but of everything happening around them. People were packing into the stands. It was like a fashion parade. Women dressed in spring dresses, some with gloves, hats, and sun parasols, took their places in box seats. Men were dressed in suits, ties, and even a few sported top hats! Faye proudly sat in her print flowered dress, excited but also very content. Smiling to herself, Faye broke the silence between them, *"My, isn't this a splendid day!"*

Hearing the first strains of *My Old Kentucky Home*, there came a sudden hush over the crowd. The big race was about to begin. Everyone stood to join in. *"The sun shines bright on my old Kentucky home."* The horses entered the track parading by, one by one, number by number. One last chance to look for a winner. Faye spotted her gray: Hartack wore a red cap. She nodded, thinking, "I have a good bet." Jockey's dressed in their brightly colored silks held their spirited mounts tightly. Their colors whipped gently in the wind as they galloped in stride to, *"Weep no more my lady, Oh weep no more today!"*

Faye had never felt the way she did at this moment. The Derby was everything she expected it to be and more. The traditions and colors couldn't be matched. The horses were great. The excitement was terrific. Being with George made it perfect. She felt so thrilled, a tear trickled down her rogue-colored cheek. George, too, knew this was right. Smiling like he only smiled at Faye, "My dear Faye, Happy Anniversary." They squeezed each other tight. And with the last refrain, *"For my old Kentucky home, far away,"* the nostalgic hold on the crowd gave way to the frenzy of last-minute wagering.

Within a few minutes, the event so long anticipated would be over. With a rush, every horse was led into the starting gate, and for only an instant they all stood ready. The beginning bell sounded, and all jumped out of the shoots. Hearts pumped to the beat. Long shots, Sharp Count and Lee Town, took early leads before giving way to favorite, Sunrise County. Ridan held steady off the lead. On the far turn and across the field, fans strained to see their favorite. Faye couldn't see her gray. She could see two or three red caps, one with his horse running last! Coming into the backstretch, hoofbeats rumbled, then nearing, they thundered! The earth and stands seemed to tremble. Fans rushed to the fence cheering and shouting. The noise of the crowd swept to a quick crescendo. Suspense electrified the air!

Now, Faye could see her gray coming to the outside. Hartack was letting him go. Nose to nose. For the split seconds to the finish, Faye might as well have been on that horse. She caught the cadence of his stride. She felt his surging energy. Faye willed that gray to win. Chanting "Go! Go! Go!," her body powered two-fisted motions to the rhythm of the jockey's whip. Across the finish line, Hartack riding Decidedly won the race. Not only did he win the race, but he had run the Derby faster than any horse before, breaking the great Whirlaway's 1941 record. Decidedly, only the second gray to ever win the Derby, and a long shot, paid $19.40 to win.

Anything else that happened that day you might imagine would seem of little consequence. Yet one more part to this story remains vivid. George vowed that when they left Churchill Downs he was going to get out of the "damn city" as soon as possible. They would go with the traffic flow no matter the direction. And so they did! Straight south. The map was no longer important. Anytime George found a road that would take them out of traffic, he would make a quick turn. And they drove. Finding a gravel road, not much traffic now! The sun went down, and a glance at the gas tank gauge indicated it did, too. Yet the car rumbled on. Dad was mad; Mother, a bit amused, remained silent. Finally, a road sign appeared. Mother squinted to read it as the lights reflected on the small dirt-covered sign, "Ten miles to ... Rome!" George took an even tighter grip on the wheel and pushed the gas pedal even harder. Neither knew how long the old Ford ran on empty, but it did get them to a motel that night. Somewhere. They never did tell.

Every year thereafter, George and Faye retold the story. Each had their version, every year a bit different. Often you would hear Faye say, "There's just nothing like the Derby." Every May we knew where Faye's mind and heart would be. I would ask, "Mom, who are you betting on this year?" She would chuckle a little and quickly reply, "The winner, of course."

What stories do your parents always tell?
What stories of your life are most important to you now? Tell them to others.
Record them!

One of many roadside picnics.

APRIL

Dear Ruth,

I have often been asked, "How did your dad ever have so much time for all his hobbies?" Think about it. Dad's basketball accident made a big difference to all of our lives, especially Mother's. Sometimes Dad could not be on his ulcerated feet to do cafe work. This would tend to get him away from the cafe routine, and, therefore, he was relatively free to come and go from the Wishmore as he pleased. Everyone waited on Dad: his Mother, our Mother, sometimes you, and sometimes me.

At home, father and mother roles were traditional. It was o.k. for Dad to be in the kitchen at the Wishmore, but not at home. I never saw him wash dishes anywhere. So, with all of this, it was Mother who kept the day-to-day business going and also the household. Nevertheless, I never knew a time when Mother wasn't devoted to Dad and he to her. We have never talked about this, but did you see this any differently? To me, she followed Dad's changing interests with keen enthusiasm. She was with him from ham radio, to photography, model railroading, tropical fish, and whatever else.

Mother was always optimistic and my cheerleader. I recall that when I was old enough to begin working at the cafe, the only time I could find time to practice my trumpet was early morning before I left for school, or at least that's how I looked at it. Dad would complain about this, because he slept later in the morning after working at the cafe late into the night. Mother said, "Well, George, if Janice is working, that's the only time she will have to practice." It wasn't long, however, before my work hours changed; so did my practice hours!

I will always be amazed how Mother found time to support our efforts and work as well. The diploma for my doctorate sitting on Mother's piano was a constant reminder of all this. Mother would often say, "Janice, don't you want to take your diploma and hang it in your office?" And I would respond, "It is as much yours as it is mine." For every diploma and award I ever received, a part of Mother was in it. When I went to Indiana University to defend my dissertation, Mom and Dad went with me. I met with my committee, and they asked me to revise a chapter. Rather than going home, we stayed to make the needed changes. Over the next few days, I drank a lot of coffee, Dad ate ice cream, and Mother sat in the motel and typed. So it was and had always been.

So, Ruth, it was Mother's support underlying everything else that glued us together. Her spirit and her energy shined through, better than any sunny summer day.

Until I see you again, take care.

Janice

Find Mother's watch pin, twice! Her neighborhood stitchery. Kilkare Club women at 604 Locust. Can you see her candlewick goblets and dishes on her lace tablecloth?

Dear Jan,

Our Mother was something of an angel in disguise. Do you remember that in the eulogy for her these angelic ways were expressed?

"She was a friend. She was our best friend. She was there for us. She gave of herself endlessly and unselfishly. She applauded our every achievement, encouraged our every struggle, consoled our every worry, defended us to the end. She had the wisdom of ages inside her. She loved music and flowers and children—the beautiful things of life. She delighted in the beauty of nature and was always looking up to see and hear the sights and sounds that the world gives us. She taught us many things— how to laugh, how to live — how to die."

Anyone could see that angel coming out in her smile, her eyes, and her quick response to things that needed to be done the right way. No wonder she had the energy and the wisdom to stay with you and type, so you could think and revise your dissertation. If you think about it, Mom was very well focused on the task to be done. Yet, she never lost sight of the big picture. Her support and interest in education was evident in so many ways. As a young woman, she supported the local schools by knowing the needs of the teachers. She helped them all she could. Knowing that they were paid only once a month, she and Dad were generous in giving them a charge account at the cafe, so they would pay just once a month.

When we were children, she saw to it that we met the requirements necessary for our education and supported the teachers in what they were trying to do for us. At the cafe, they liked the after school teacher crowd for coffee and pie. They made sure to stay open after the ball games to accommodate the enthusiasm with sandwiches and malts. Our parents knew that the school was a main hub of activity in the small town of La Porte City.

As a grandmother, Mom was always interested in the grandchildren's education, talking to them about it, encouraging them, and dropping a few words of advice along the way. She was there when they performed in extracurricular events, applauding and enjoying the times she may have missed with us because of her work at the cafe. As I am finding out now and as she knew much earlier, grandparenting is sort of a "second chance" to do it all again.

I understand what you are saying about the support Mom gave you with your graduate education. When I went off to work on another degree, she said, "You are never too old to learn." She knew that I wanted to learn more about child development and could use it well in my teaching experience. She knew how hard it was for me to start something new and also deal with a growing family. One semester, she rode to night class with me. She didn't want me to travel alone. As we traveled the road to Ames, she tapped her foot to the radio music and enjoyed the beautiful sunsets. She was a trooper. We hustled along to grab a bite to eat and then headed to class. She sat in class with me! The college students and the professor were very impressed by her support and interest. A letter came to her after class was over describing the appreciation the professor had for her support of education. I am not sure that you ever saw the letter Professor Herwig sent to Mother, so I am sending a copy to you.

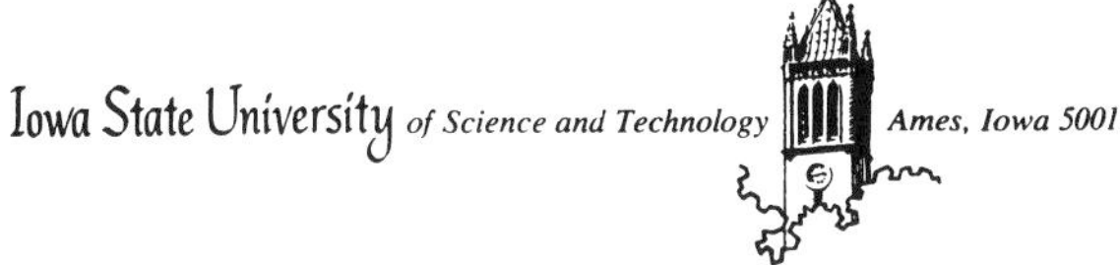

Child Development Department
101 Child Development Building
Telephone 515-294-3040

January 6, 1987

Dear Mrs. Abel,

When Ruth walks across the platform to receive her M.S. degree, I certainly hope there is room for you in her pocket or in her footsteps! You are a very impressive mother in the ways you are being supportive of Ruth's graduate education and welfare. The CD 525 students and I were envious of the support you exhibited for Ruth! And you even made treats for all of us! I certainly would be more at ease with Ruth's long Tuesday night drives to Ames knowing that you were accompanying her. Again, thanks and bouquets to you!!

Best wishes in the new year.

Sincerely,

Joan E. Herwig, Ph.D.
Associate Professor

Faye's letter from Professor Herwig reads as follows.

Dear Mrs. Abel,

When Ruth walks across the platform to receive her M. S. degree, I certainly hope there is room for you in her pocket or in her footsteps! You are a very impressive mother in the ways you are being supportive of Ruth's graduate education and welfare. The CO 525 students and I were envious of the support you exhibited for Ruth! And you even made treats for all of us! I certainly could be more at ease with Ruth's long Tuesday night drives to Ames knowing that you were accompanying her. Again, thanks and bouquets to you!

Best Wishes in the new year.

Sincerely,

Joan E. Herwig, Ph. D.

Associate Professor

I hope springtime is coming soon. The warm sunshine, singing birds, and blooming flowers pour memories of Mother into my mind. From season to season, Mother saw to it that we participated in the events. With every special event, with each Halloween popcorn ball, or new Easter outfit, every frilly May basket or smell of pumpkin pie, I will be reminded of Mother.

I sure miss her sweet smile and warm ways—but I will always have her in my heart. There she will be, applauding us, laughing with us, encouraging us, consoling us.

Hope to see you soon. Don't forget to stop and smell the roses!!

Love, Ruth Anne

P.S. I am enclosing a recipe for caramel popcorn. Mom and I enjoyed making this for years. It's easy and so tasty—try it sometime. I am also sending you this poem. So often when I see a beautiful sunset, I think of Mom. I was so impressed with the sunset when I wrote this poem.

Record special stories about your mother.
Describe her. When you think of your mother, what do you see her doing? Where?
As a child, what activities did you do together?
What objects and words do you associate
with your mother?

God has surely used his paintbrush
    upon this sky so blue.
For there upon he's blended
    pastel colors of every hue.
He's gently layered colors
    across the spacious sky
T'would be a task impossible
    for either you or I
Some colors shimmer brightly
    from sunset's last warm light
Some are soft and cool as a whisper
    before the dark blue of night
With every stroke he's kissed the world
    And with this unending love
Reminds us of his masterpiece
    created from above.

SUMMER, 1977

To: Ruth
From: Janice

Ruth, your letter jolted my awareness about education. I wondered why we hadn't talked much about school in our letter writing. Of course, it wasn't school that made us hungry for learning. It was Mom and Dad supporting learning everywhere! Even if Mother was busy during the day, she would always read a bedtime story to me. A favorite of mine was *Peter Rabbit* and also some of the traditional Christmas stories. Mom and Dad had magazines lying around the house all the time. Mother had her *Better Homes and Garden Magazine*, and Dad had his *QST Magazine* (amateur radio). Remember getting our set of encyclopedias and a companion set of Junior Classics? I think we must have read the words off the pages. Very vivid in my mind is the time I went through each volume of the encylopedia and identified all the universities and colleges in the United States. I drew a United States map and located each college using a classification system for private and public institutions. That's when I realized I wanted to go to college.

As I became interested in music, my life became centered around school activities, classes, favorite teachers, and classmates. I have found many pictures of us in high school activities, whereas only a few related to grade school. I doubt very much if we ever had many pictures. Enclosed is a picture of our school building on Commercial Street. Send along any pictures you find. I am going to rummage through some more of the black and white snapshots Dad had stashed in the old cigar boxes.

Until I see you next,

Love, Jan

Notes about school days. What did your school look like?
Who were your teachers? Your friends?
Pick one experience about school and write about it in as much detail as possible.
Can you recall who said what?

La Porte Highschool / Grade School. See map, page 101.
Below, the corner stone.

MAY

Dear Jan,

I did not find any pictures from elementary school either. You know, school was our "work." We looked forward to weekends so that we could play and have fun. Dad's photography included home settings and community activities. In those days, parents wouldn't think of intruding into the school for pictures.

The weekends came, and of course Friday night was movie night. Saturday night was a hot night on Main Street, and all the country folks came to town to visit with one another. I had fun getting ready to go uptown on Saturday night. I would wait on the front steps for Grandma Abel to go with us up the street to Main Street. Mom was working at the cafe, and Grandma and Grandpa Burrows would be coming to town to spend the evening. We had fun sitting in their Hudson (the first car that you could "step down into") and watching the people walk down the street. Grandma and Sharon, our cousin, and I would sit in the car and make interesting comments about the people passing by. I can still hear my Grandma chuckling about the way a particular lady walked and talked or how her dress was swishing this way and that.

The heat of the day was whisked away with a cool evening breeze. The night bugs gathered at the neon lights of the cafe. Our cafe was one of the first to have neon lights. By then the cafe had already been remodeled to add more seating at the counter and a set of 5 booths in the back. This became the gathering place for many families and friends. The chatter in the cafe and all up and down the street on Saturday night kept our little town of La Porte City buzzing. During the '30s and '40s, people talked of the war and how to save and how to use the rations. Many concessions were made to accommodate the hard times during the war. The thing that stands out to me were the blackouts. We had to practice in case of an invasion. I would grab my pillow and wait for the lights to come back on. Being kids, we hardly knew the significance of what we were doing. We lived in a protected world where we could run and play. The war things were just part of our daily routine that as far as we were concerned might go on forever. The fact that gas and sugar were rationed was not a hardship on us. Shoes were rationed, and we always got our new pair when we had the ration coupons for them. Mother said that we probably had more shoes during that time than in later years! We went to Walkers in Waterloo to buy them. I liked the X-ray machine where I could look down at my wiggling toes to see if the shoe fit well. The hard times didn't mean much to us. We were a family, and that was all that mattered.

What do you remember about our early childhood at the cafe? You write next. I have school activities every night this week! Wow! I hope I have the energy!

Your little sister,

Ruth Anne

Notes about uptown, shopping, special nights. Is this before or after TV?

Dowtown Saturday night.

To calm a busy day, to ease an aching heart
to make all things seem pleasant, and right again to start
I need only to let my thoughts carry me back from today,
to childhood — and the taste of yesterday.

The first sound that comes to me on yesterday's still air
Is the sound of the locusts, as I, a child, sit on our porch stair.

I sit in crisp ironed dress and skin soaped soft and clean.
I love the click of new shiny shoes and blue satin sash so sheen.
I love the fresh feel of the cool night breeze upon my silky hair.
Then the stillness —
And the sound of the locust to soothe my childhood care

The day had been filled with play and bikes and sun,
With sand and bare feet, sweat and pig-tailed fun.
The soft summer rain has cooled the night just right.
And now we look forward to Uptown Saturday Night!

But just now I'll sit and listen and feel and taste the air.
Oh, may I never forget the sound and smell
As I sit here on the porch stair.

And now I'm grown,
A warm summer day is filled
with work and golf and sun,
with gardens and dirt, bare feet,
and rose-picking fun.

Somehow I know by the pounding in my chest,
the lump in my throat, the tear swelling in my eye,
That these are all God's guarantee. Forget?
Never, Never will I.

Oh, how I relish the nights when the soft breeze comes,
And the childhood thoughts it brings.
The night when the wind smells of roses,
and the locust sings!

SUMMER 1971

To: Ruth
From: Janice

Ruth, I just had this thought. You talked about rationing and the war effort. All of these things were the norm for us growing up. We didn't know anything different. I recall the blackouts and how I wanted to be sure and have every light out so the enemy in their airplanes would never see our house! I doubt that you ever heard me tell the story about my first grade teacher, Miss Scott, who married an air pilot in the service and became Mrs. Weller. The very next year, having myself moved on to second grade, Lt. Weller was reported missing in action. Mrs. Weller was so upset that she left teaching in the middle of the school year. It caused quite a turmoil for the whole school. The principal came to all the grades to tell us the bad news. The song "Coming in on a Wing and a Prayer" reverberated in my life throughout the war reminding me of Mrs. Weller and her Lieutenant. Anytime we heard a plane, I was reminded of the pilot; anytime we heard a plane I looked to see if it had the right markings for the USA! For me, a six year old living in the middle of the USA, this made the war become very real!

Now, in my adulthood, I realize how naive we all were at the time with all the atrocities happening in other parts of the world.

To Ruth
From: Jan

Look at this great picture I found of the family! Even though picnics are an important part of Midwest summer fun, and even though this picture portrays the relaxed serene life of a family on a summer day, I look at this picture and wonder how it would have happened in our family. For any of us to get in the scene would have been difficult. We all would have considered it a very special time. I know this must have happened on Grandpa and Grandma Burrows farm because the chair Grandpa is sitting on was kept in the shed where they separated cream from fresh milk. The car with the door standing open probably belonged to Uncle Glen and Aunt Frances. They were just beginning to farm on their own. They were always scrambling to get somewhere. Then there was Aunt Nina and Uncle Harry (standing at the end of the table). Nina worked for the folks, and Harry could easily have just come from his work at the La Porte City Utilities. And the folks, I don't know how they could have ever been to a picnic. Most any day they would have been at the Wishmore. Understandably, both Grandmas look very pleased and grateful about having the family together. I must have spied Dad taking this picture, because I am looking directly at the camera. Cousin Glenda is sitting beside me, but where are you, Ruth? And cousins Sharon and Marilyn? I can imagine that you three were off playing somewhere—in the sandbox, in the barn, or on the swing. One thing I do recall was the great ice cream grandpa made. He made it with fresh thick cream, packed in ice, and wrapped in gunnysack. His ice cream was so different than Wishmore ice cream—softer, whiter and colder! I bet you three joined the scene when the ice cream was served!

For living in a rural community, it didn't seem like we spent much time on the farm. Anytime before I went to the farm, Mom and Dad gave me a lecture, "Stay away from the machinery. Do not get on the tractor. Don't get close the the hog lot, and stay clear of the horses." Now, pray tell, what would there be left for me to do on the farm? I especially felt left out because cousins Sharon, Marilyn, and Glenda lived on a farm and knew all the ropes. They knew how to feed the hogs, drive the horses, and collect chicken eggs without getting pecked. They would get over a fence in a split second, and I would be left standing on the other side. The town kid couldn't cut the mustard.

For me, the most memorable time on the farm was a much earlier year on a summer day. Grandma took Glenda and me for a picnic lunch to the field where Grandpa was working. Glenda hadn't yet got infantile paralysis, so I imagine we weren't much more than 6 or 7. We went barefoot, and for me that was a treat because rarely did I go barefoot at home. Grandpa took a break, and we ate our lunch parked on a large log. Grandma brought out a red checkered cloth and spread it out, and we ate sandwiches and drank lemonade from a large tin cup.

We were about to leave when all of a sudden Grandpa picked me up and in a declaring voice said, "You have to have a ride on a tractor." And with that, he sat me on his lap, and with the putt, putt sound of the tractor, we were off! I had never felt so tall. I was above the field and felt like I was almost to the sky. The corn was short; I think we were cultivating,

and as we passed along, it was amazing how straight the patterns of corn! A checkered pattern. No matter the angle, each corn stock was part of a row. The sky was so wide! Turning full circle, it looked like each row of corn went 'til it met the sky—big and blue with frothy white meringue clouds floating by. I put my hand on the steel steering wheel; Grandpa's hand was so big and dark compared to mine. I could smell the summer dust, his sweat, and the faint scent of barnyard on his overalls, but surprisingly, it smelled awfully clean. Too soon the ride was over. I felt guilty for a long time about not telling Mom and Dad about my tractor ride, but I could hardly wait to get back to the farm again. I just loved it.

City slicker, no way! Still, today I will go an extra hundred miles to avoid a city, and go an extra thousand to ride through rolling hills of corn and wheat and to catch a glimpse of the sun setting across an Iowa pond.

Let's go for a picnic.

Janice

To Jan:

I love the picnic picture! It is a true Midwestern snapshot, one that could be taken of many farm families—but this was *our* family! I was thinking that perhaps it was a holiday—Memorial Day, the 4th of July, or Labor Day. Some of the holidays, our parents would be closed for part of the day, giving them an opportunity to spend time with their family. They were closed on Thursdays, too. Maybe this was a Thursday.

I'm sure that Sharon and Marilyn and I were off playing in the barn—probably searching out a family of kittens. I always liked hearing their sweet little mews coming out of the haymow, and I loved the sweet smell of the hay in the barn. You may have secretly loved the farm, and I guess I did, too.

I liked going to Grandma's for a day or two. She made the best fried chicken, wonderfully crispy on the outside and tender middles. We played in many rooms of their house, but I liked the kitchen the best. Grandpa would come in from chores in his baggy overalls. He was delighted to see us, and on seeing us there in the kitchen playing with the little iron wagon and horses, he would draw our attention by immediately going into a dancing jig. He must have had a little Irish in him.

After supper Sharon and Marilyn and I would play outside for a while. That big twisted tree in the yard was a great gathering place. Then after dark we would go inside to play. Farm families usually went to bed early, so we would go upstairs to share a small bedroom. I'll never forget the first time I stayed overnight—when lights went out. I was totally shocked by the darkness. Being a town girl, there had always been street lights or something to create light in the darkness of our bedroom—but not in the country!! "Sharon! Marilyn! Are you there?" "Yes," they giggled. I pulled the covers up to my chin and opened my eyes wider thinking it would help me see in the dark. "I can't see anything!! Even with my eyes open wider!" They giggled again. I'm sure they told everybody about the plight of the city girl in the darkness.

I'll take you up on the picnic. I know we'll have a mild sunny day soon. I'll bring the fried chicken and the hot chocolate. You bring the potato salad and the ice cream!

Ruth Anne

What stories do you recall about places with which you were not familiar
or comfortable. City? Country?

JULY

Dear Ruth,

The photo I have enclosed of you sitting at the counter must have been taken in 1942 or 1943 considering your size. There you are, sitting at the counter like you would have been most any day. Do you remember Floyd, the guy with the pencil stuck under his hat? He was the D and D man who came every week or two to supply us with foodstuff. He would come in, have a cup of coffee, and spend time with the locals before taking the pencil from his hat and saying in a business-like manner, "George, what do you need today? We have chips on special with an order of 2 or more boxes of peanuts."

"Fill the post up with a combination of chips and popcorn," Dad would reply, pointing to the center post. "The jar of peanuts is almost empty again, too. Fill it up," he'd say, looking at me, and smiling just a little. "Someone's been in the peanuts again."

I wouldn't look at Dad. I knew he was talking about me. It was hard to keep it a secret. A Planters Peanut breath was always hard to hide. Soon Floyd would be behind the counter, thumb tacking the chips to the large center post. The job done, he would turn around. "Back in a couple of weeks," he would say. "Now, Janice, you be good," and he'd give me a quick wink. "Don't eat too many peanuts!" And out the door he would go.

It would never be very long, after opening at 5:00 a.m., before the door would open and a parade of locals would line the counter, starting a typical day at the Wishmore. Hank Kruse, the town Marshall, the only guy in town with a gun on his belt, would sidle up to the counter holding a big cigar. "Why did he ever take those boys out? No wonder we lost this one," he'd exclaim.

"It wasn't the coach's fault," someone would retort. "Our kids are doing great. All the first starters are freshmen this year. After all, Vinton won the sectional title last year."

"I'm not talking about baseball. I'm talking about General Eisenhower. Those soldiers didn't have a chance and…" chewing on his cigar, he muttered on. Listening seriously to all of this, you could have thought worldly decisions were made right here at the counter in La Porte City, Iowa! Momentarily, I might be caught thinking, "Gee!" Then soon, I would just smile to myself and tune it all out. It was, however, the daily counter bantering that most often led to my enthusiasm for the next town celebration or upcoming basketball game.

Ruth, look at the full pie case in the photo. I can imagine Aunt Nina and Mother having arrived at the cafe before the sun came up to make pies. This picture had to be taken rather early in the day, or the pie case would have been empty.

The noon whistle signaled a pretty set script. Doc Bailey would soon arrive. If you looked down the street, you would see this slender man wearing a white shirt, with a neat bow tie, holding a pipe tightly in his teeth, briskly walking toward the cafe. He entered with a dramatic, "Hello," and gesture to the pie case. "Hey, Fa-aye. Grab me a piece of that apple pie." Sitting down, laying his pipe on the counter, he would lean over a little as Faye took the pie from the case, "And put a little cheddar on it, ok?"

The strangers at the counter learned their parts fast. Before you knew it, they all had ordered a piece of pie, many with a slice of cheese along the side. I often wondered about the many ways Doc helped all of us on Main. It really came home to me years later, when I was about to start college. I was pretty nervous about it all, and about leaving home. Doc came in as usual; he was smiling an extra big smile on this day. "So, you are off to college! Well, what will we do without you? Not too many miles away though. Come back and serve me pie once in a while, o.k.? Here, Jannie," and he pushed a paper into my sweaty palm and rushed out the door. I gripped it tightly and slowy opened the crumple piece—a one hundred dollar bill! I had never seen one before!

Ruth,when I look at this counter picture, I see a place and people braced for business. Everything was in order. Even when I was very young, I begged Dad to let me help. I couldn't reach the cigars, but Dad let me refill the cigarette case. They were 20 cents a pack. In the picture, you can see the popular ones: Camel, Kool, Lucky Strike. The pipe tobacco was in cans, showing just above the cigarettes, and the cigars higher yet in their fancy boxes. I especially liked putting in the Wing Cigarettes because each pack included a picture card of a World War II airplane much like sports cards of today.

I relished keeping the candy case filled. Notice in the photo the cases are located on either side of the cash register. Keeping the pop cooler filled was difficult, especially when we were busy. Remember the rule? When we took a bottle out, we had to replace it. Too often, we got busy and forgot the rule. Keeping counter items, sugar, salt and pepper, napkins, straws, and toothpicks filled was always fun, and taking them out and using the straws and toothpicks was always tempting.

Night would come, and all was ready. Like a scout sent ahead of the crowd, a single customer bursting in the door might announce, "We won 8 to 7 in the 10th inning." Soon on his heels, the door would open and fans, coaches, and players in uniforms poured into the place. Customers scrunched into the five booths. Men and women scrambled for the counter seats, some twirling around on the stools that revolved like merry-go-rounds. Completing the packed place were people standing in back of the seated counter customers to order take-outs. Sometimes the lines extended to the outside.

Dad took the counter; there was always a high school girl to serve the booths; Marlys or Mary, maybe Virginia. I stood ready at the sandwich-making counter. Mom was the commander, coordinator, and chief cook. Orders flooded in.

"Order up," Mary would cry, "5 burgers and fries." And then another and another.

Dad would shout, "Hey, make me some fries."

People were laughing and chattering about the home run hits or maybe the ones that struck out. In the background, you could hear someone yelling for another soda, or "Hey, George, I need another refill." The fries frizzled; the hamburgers sizzled, and as soon as nickels hit the slot on the Jukebox, we could hear above this all the Andrew sisters singing "The Boogie, Woogie Bugle Boy from Company B." The rhythm was terrific. We all became animated; it must have been a sight to see!

In the midst of all this, I would always think it, and often blurt out, "We're in a jam, aren't we, Mom?..."

"Hey, get me a coke, will you, Jannie," Mary asked as she grabbed silverware, hot drinks, and maybe some pie.

I filled the counter with open buns. I kept scrunching more on to get them ready for the burgers to come. Ketchup, mustard, pickles, and I always hoped not onions—they made me cry.

"You have a bit of mustard on your nose," Dad might say grinning, not missing a beat in packing the sacks for carry out. I was hot; my hands were flying on automatic. I didn't care about a little mustard. I shrugged it off, and smiled back. I felt like I could go on forever.

"George, we need a couple of malts. Janice, get pickles on those buns." Mom would keep us going.

And once again Mary came flying by, "Order up, two steaks and American fries."

"Darn," Mom would say shaking her head. This broke the rhythm. The American fries had to be cooked elsewhere on the stove, and the steak on the grill intruded on the burgers.

This was the signal for me to run back to the old ice box and grab a jello salad and an order of bread, two slices with a quarter size square of butter.

"Hey, we're running out of cold pop," Dad would shout.

I dashed to the front under the counter where the pop in wooden cases were stacked, grabbed as many bottles as I could, and opened the cooler door. Yu-uck! All that was left was the gooey paper pop labels sloshing around in the water. Won't these pop companies ever learn not to glue on paper labels? What a mess! I knew cleaning the pop cooler would be somebody's job that night; I hoped it wasn't mine! I plopped in the pop and closed the door.

With the sound of the cash register beginning to ring, I knew we were winning this jam session for the night. The squeaky-clean dishes that had been neatly stacked on the front shelves had now been shifted to the back wash counter in a tossed and tumbled manner with leftovers smashed between. As suddenly as people poured in, they poured out. At the counter there might be a few businessmen sipping cups of coffee before going home. If we were lucky, the nickelodeon would still be playing.

"So, what about this mustard on my nose," I mused, pointing to Dad's big white apron — ketchup, mustard, chocolate splatters, and a little meringue on the side. Mom would laugh outloud, and so would I. Now, all that was left was to make the place picture perfect again.

Wow, what memories! Ruth, only one more thing before I close. Do you remember the Jukebox? It held the big disks with a pencil-sized hole. Speed 78! Only ten or twelve selections! We always had a Gene Autry on it, and the tunes the big bands brought to us, the Dorsey brothers, Harry James, and Les Brown with his "band of renown." During the holidays, "I'll Be Home for Christmas" or Bing Crosby's "White Christmas" played until the last customer left. The busy cafe chatter mixed with the pop tunes had a sound like none I have heard since.

Ruth, I'm sending you the photo. Do share with me your recollections of this time. Guess I'll have hamburgers tonight with a little cheese along the side.

Love, Janice!

AUGUST

Dear Jan,

Details of the picture you sent are things I remember but not in the way you do. I was probably about 5 or even 6. The customers and the delivery guys always asked me when I was going to start to school, and I had already started! What an insult!

I picture Dad behind the counter talking to customers. He had time to talk — unless he was called to the kitchen to help sling hamburgers. I remember many of those times when everyone was running as fast as they could to keep up with business. Don't you wonder how Mom did it? She must have had a lot of energy. When she had to go to the basement to haul up cases of pop, she grabbed them by the pop bottles and took one in each hand up the stairs.

Some of the things I liked most about the cafe were my favorite pop, cream soda, and taking an ice cream bar whenever I wanted one. I especially liked to put 7Up in the malt machine to take the fizz out of it—guess I thought it tasted better. The sounds and smells are etched in my mind. I can still hear the squeak of the front door when someone entered, the sound of the cash register, the busyness of the place. I can smell the pop cooler, the dishwasher soap, the cooking food.

We had a wide range of customers, from those we knew well on a daily basis to those who might drop in every year on vacation, to a stranger we would only see once. With some customers, the clock could have been kept. If someone didn't show up, we wondered what was wrong and what had happened. It wasn't long before we would know, as news traveled fast on Main Street.

I am sure you remember a particular night when we were cleaning up after another busy day. We had cleaned off the grill, taken out the trash, and were patiently waiting for the last customer to leave so we could go home. Dad came in from burning the trash. "Well, that's about it. Are we about ready to go home?" Mom looked up, drying the last piece of silverware. Nodding towards the counter, she said, "We have one customer left at the counter." We all looked in unison. At the counter sat Mr. Earl Bagley with his hat on eating a pork chop. I know the pork chops were delicious, but he was enjoying it ferociously. The earflaps of his hat were flopping around as he was gnawing and tearing the last bits of meat off the bone. He was almost growling as his greasy fingers held the bone tight up the side of his face. We all stood silently, and then suddenly burst into a chorus of laughter. Mr. Earl Bagley didn't even notice. Etiquette was not one of Mr. Bagley's high points!

Another regular customer was Charlie, the town drunk. Do you remember him as vividly as I do, Jan? I especially remember a busy Friday night, when Charlie was sitting at the counter. Dad had tolerated Charlie's drunken presence and had served his food quickly, hoping he would leave with no problem. The counter was lined with hungry chattering customers. A group of high school girls were giggling and sipping on malt straws. But as the business increased and no attention was paid to Charlie, he decided to get close to the girls, leaving his food sitting half-eaten at the counter. "Well, little girly," he sloshed, "are ya havin' any fun?" His reddened, watery eyes peered longingly at the young girls' fair skin. Both girls reeled with astonishment and moved away without a word of response. Charlie inched himself on to the next counter stool and, again, to another young girl, "How about a little kiss?" he slurred. She very quickly pushed him away with a loud, "No!" Being rather unbalanced anyway, it didn't take much of a push to send him to the floor in a heap. He slowly retorted, "Well, ya don't have ta push a guy down, do ya?" He lay there contemplating his next move, as the girls left the counter and went out the door in a rush. As soon as Dad was alerted to the disturbance, he told Charlie, "Get up and get out!" That began a shouting match, and Dad had little patience for that kind of thing. Even though Dad was small, he was strong and strong willed. Charles was lying near the door. Dad managed to take him by the back of the collar and the seat of the pants and literally throw him out the door. Mom was there to pick up his hat and throw it out after him, and they both went back to work hardly skipping a beat!

There are many more stories to tell about customers, and this is one I have shared with my children. Perhaps you remember this next one as well.

It was a typical summer afternoon in La Porte City. The door squeaked open, and the hot air blew in along with Harold Morgan. Harold was a small, prim fellow wearing a cotton striped shirt and summer trousers held up with striped suspenders. He was a plain little man, always rather quiet, and very regular with his order of his afternoon snack before going home for the day. He sat down as usual on the revolving counter stool. Mom was busy wiping the other end of the counter and had just noticed his presence from the corner of her eye. She stepped back to the kitchen to get a glass of water for him and then brought it quickly to the counter. As she set the water before him, she glanced into his face to take his order. "May I help you?" she said. At that very moment, she noticed the bright bit of color on Harold's head. She looked again, as he replied, "The usual." She bit her lip to squelch a laugh. "Oh, yes, let's see, apple pie with a small scoop of vanilla ice cream, coffee with cream and sugar." He nodded, not realizing a butterfly was perched on his head. The bright bit of color was apparently enjoying the hair oil on the sleek hair. Mom turned quickly to avoid laughing in his face. Before filling the order, she had to whisper this little bit of humor to the kitchen help. She prepared the pie and coffee and served it with laughter almost bursting from her smiling face. "Aren't we cheerful today?" remarked Harold. "Yes," she responded, "things are all a flutter around here." Now, the girls in the kitchen were peeking out of the serving window with mouth-covered giggles. Harold sat peacefully enjoying his pie and coffee, smiling, too, and wondering what was so amusing. "Well, back to work girls," Mom said with a twinkle in her eye.

Mother told this story to the family many times, and everytime she did, I could see the glitter in all of our eyes.

The other day when I was talking to my La Porte City friends about the cafe, they mentioned the pies. When people think of the cafe, they always mention the pies. It was a big drawing card for customers. Mom and Nina became very good pie-makers and were willing to try to make most any kind for variety. The apple pie, however, was the staple and the favorite of many. Mom made many cream pies—most with a meringue topping. She made walnut cream, banana cream, pineapple cream, coconut cream, raisin cream, apple cream, lemon, custard, and, of course, chocolate. That wasn't all by any means, but these were the most usual. I have enclosed some pie recipes that came from Mom's cookbook you might like to try.

With all the customers and activities on Main, wasn't it great that we were able to close and take a vacation? Vacations were one thing we all looked forward to and worked hard for all year. The customers complained about us being gone for *2 weeks!* We wondered if they would come back, but they always did.

Until I see you next, Love, Ruth Anne

George takes a break and talks city business with grocer Max
Thomspson from across the street.

What family photos tell your story? Begin by selecting one and describe it in detail.
Share it with others. What stories or experiences come to mind?
Select others and build a journal of photos
and related experiences.

AUGUST

Dear Jan,

I am happy you are off to Texas for an early vacation. It's good to have a break from the regular routine. Even though we don't see each other a lot when you are here, I miss you when you are gone. I will soon be going off to Texas myself. It seems that vacations became a part of our regular activities early in our lives. I recall Dad would often say, "When we can stack silver dollars to the ceiling (he would place a few on the floor next to the corner cupboard), we will take a trip." I can still hear the silver dollars click on the table as they were counted, and I dreamed of the day those dollars would reach the ceiling! I am sure the dollars were never stacked to the ceiling, but the trips did become reality.

Vacations with our parents started with many preparations. Dad would buy a new road atlas and study it in great detail, knowing all the main roads we would take by the time we were ready to go. Even though AAA might provide him with a triptic for a route, Dad would have alternatives. Dad never liked going into cities; he would drive an extra 100 miles to avoid them, although I do remember times when we took tours of cities like Washington D.C., Boston, and Quebec. A favorite place was Colorado, but over the years Dad would plan to go to different places, and eventually our family did touch on all of the 48 continental states. Those were great family trips.

The first vacation remains vivid in my memory. It was in 1947 for a week at Spring Lake near Muskegon, Michigan. Having no idea how much to take, we filled big suitcases with almost everything we owned. In fact, the suitcases were the ones that came with our flirting-eyed dolls, don't you remember? However, I'm sure we learned soon what was important and what was not necessary to take. The car, of course, was not air conditioned, and we had the windows down with our hair blowing in the wind to stay cool. We didn't mind—the vacation was a wonderful adventure as vacations should be.

Do you remember the little round suitcase that Dad carried his film in? He was prepared for vacation if he had his maps and his camera equipment. Mom was responsible for everything else. Not only did she prepare lunch and snack items, she also made a list of items to take and made sure they were all in the car. Even on short trips in recent years, Mom brought along sandwiches and pickles! I have found her travel journals with a few notes she began writing in 1952. Each year she added more information to her journals about the trip. She kept mileage and expense records as well as comments about the day's adventures. In 1955 we went to Colorado with our aunt and uncle and stayed in the Big Spruce cabins at Idaho Springs. The cabin rent was $10.30 per night. Gas averaged about 31 cents a gallon. Dinner out in the evening for a family of four was around $3-$5. One night we spent $9.95! Mom wrote, "Wow, we really got took!"

All you and I had to do to get ready to start our trip was to get our clothes packed and our games ready for the car. It always seemed so early and a little on the cool, damp side at 4:00 a.m.! "Come on girls—get up—let's get going." Dad was already up, dressed, and having his second cup of coffee along with his first smoke of the day. Mom was pouring the coffee into the thermos. Mom had a plan for a lunch in the car, Dad had his travel plan, and we had our clothes laid out for the first day of traveling. Once awake, we dressed quickly and sat down for the toast that Mom had ready for us. "You girls make your beds and don't forget to brush your teeth. We'll be in the car for a long ride today." With a knowing nod, we were ready to go in just a few minutes. "Goodbye, Mitzi," we hugged the dog and piled into the packed car. The night air seemed strange and yet exciting for our first day of our long-awaited trip.

Do you remember the wooden two-legged table we made that fit between us in the back seat of the car? We had our stuff under the table, and we were ready to travel. You had your side, and I had mine. Watching out the window was the favorite pastime. We didn't listen to the radio much—Dad usually had his ham stuff going. We played a few games using our homemade table and had a back seat picnic. Looking for a motel was part of the fun, too. I held up three fingers to signify that the motels should be AAA rating. In those days, we didn't have reservations in advance. We just stopped when we were tired and looked for a clean place to stay. We would check the rates and look in the room before deciding if we wanted to stay or if another place would be better. There were many family-owned motels, rather than the chain-operated businesses of today. Wasn't it great to have a lot of variety and different offerings? I really liked looking in all the rooms and making a choice. I know I saved every small bar of soap from every motel we stayed in.

We stopped at many wonderful sights in the country. I was impressed with the greatness of them. Niagara Falls is mesmerizing (how much water flows over that in a day?). The Grand Canyon is enthralling. The mountains are like a breath of fresh air. I liked them all! But the ocean was the best. After admiring the glowing sunsets and the crashing waves, I always found myself searching for interesting rocks and shells. Collecting became a hobby—so every time we stopped to see a sight, I was looking for something to collect. Dad was snapping pictures, Mom was taking in the "big picture," and we were enjoying any little thing we might find. "Look there—see the chipmunk scurrying under the rocks? Let's feed it some of our crackers. Mom, can we look in those big viewers?—it just takes a nickel. Oh, look! There is a curio shop—let's go in!" I couldn't walk fast enough to get into the shop and pore over the knick knacks. Dad groaned, but got out his camera and started taking more snapshots. Mom liked the knick knacks, too. I usually left her at the post card rack. She was trying to find just the right card to send home, and I was trying to find just the "right" souvenir of the day. There is still evidence in my home of the many trips we made through gift shops from coast to coast.

So what vacations have you liked best? Recently, I guess my vacation to California with you was among my favorites. I think it is because it was a good mixture of family sight-seeing and relaxation. I like Colorado a lot, maybe because our parents liked it so much. The scenery, the mountain drives, and the smell of the pines are those things that are imprinted on my mind. My vacation to Florida with Mom in 1989 was outstanding to me. We had a great time together, and Mom was such a congenial traveler. Again we had a good mixture, the beach, horses, Disney World, and quiet fun together. I wish we could do it all over again! But I guess that is what memories and pictures are for!

Vacations can be as small as taking a break from the usual in your home—doing something different—or as grandiose as an extended tour somewhere in the world. Whichever it may be—the word vacation to me means being good to yourself!

Well, better close for now.

Be good to yourself! See you after many miles between us.

Ruth Anne

*Notes about family vacations. Have each family member relate
what was important to them about vacations.
A vacation I especially liked was ...*

Name the cowboys! What's the movie tonight? Find the original Roy Rogers mug. Center picture—find Ruth (center), cousin Norma Jean, and Marlene Buck posing for the Pigtail Contest. Even girls played with guns—find the original Gene Autry pistol.

Dear Ruth,

You said earlier that Saturday nights were special to you. Well, Friday nights were very special to me. It was movie night for most all kids in town. Marvin Foss closed the old Pastime across from the cafe in 1940 and opened the new modern Mars Theatre three blocks down Main Street.

What an opening it was! It made headlines in several area newspapers. Among congratulatory telegrams Marvin Fosse received from Hollywood stars were: From Dorothy Lamour, "Wishing you every success in the opening of your beautiful new theatre, and sincere good wishes for a long and happy career for the Mars"; From Claudette Colbert, "La Porte City should be very grateful for the new Mars theatre and I am sure it will be a success from the opening day"; From Fred MacMurray, "Here's to the new Mars. A grand opening and many happy returns for many years to come"; From Bob Hope, "It won't be long before all La Porte City will be trekking to the Mars for the great entertainment you have booked. Congratulations!"

Bob Hope was right. Much of the entertainment in La Porte City centered around movies at the Mars Theatre. On Friday nights, part of the scene was Dotty, Carol, you, and me heading for the movie. "What's the movie tonight?" I asked, even though I had a pretty good idea.

"A Roy Rogers," and strutting a little bit, you would go on to relate, "You know, King of the Cowboys." Dotty and Carol would share quick glances knowing what they were about to hear.

"But Gene Autry's the best," I would quickly respond. "You know, Mom says he is the best singer!"

"Maybe so," you would retort, "but Mom says Roy Rogers is the best actor!"

Dotty would chirp in, "Beat you all to the theatre," and then would take off running.

Nine times out of ten, JoAnn Thompson would be selling tickets. She sat in the big glass ticket window with the fancy curtains. We would shove our dime through the counter opening. "Now, let's see. All of you are under twelve, aren't you?" JoAnn would say. I wondered what I would say when I became twelve; then I would have to pay 25 cents.

We'd rush in bouncing down the carpet-cushioned aisle and take our favorite seats—far right, 2 by 2 under the second light. The older kids usually would sit in the center. Most adults would sit in the back. We'd arrive just in time. The lights would dim. The curtain would open sweeping along in a speedy motion. Now, the only beam of light we would see was the red-rimmed flashlights as latecomers were ushered to their seats. We sank back in our plush seats. They tilted to bring us face to face with the new wide silver screen. The war news came first; President Roosevelt generally had an announcement. Then, the cartoon, Bugs Bunny if we were lucky, before the main feature, a western on Friday night. Everyone cheered when the hero appeared. Tonight, not Roy and not Gene—but Hopalong Cassidy and his horse King!

Marvin held promotions at the Pastime, and now, with the new theatre he seemed to do even more. The whole Main Street was involved. Merchants would donate some goods. There was a lot of talk about the upcoming drawings, and in the hearts of many, as there are today with the lotteries, everyone dreamed of winning. One promotion, I recall, was the time Marvin gave every moviegoer an 8 x 10 photo of Roy Rogers and Dale Evans. On this occasion, Ruth, you were sick and couldn't go, so Dad told me to ask for an extra picture so you could have one. What would have been a simple task for most, shy as I was, I really wrestled with just how I would do this. I knew if I didn't ask, the picture I'd get would have to be yours. So, the night came and I bought my ticket and entered. There stood Marvin. You may recall, he was lanky and well over 6 foot. That night he even seemed taller! He was handing out the pictures. I looked up, and in a very fast, monotone voice, I managed, "My sister is sick, and may I have a picture for her, too?" *I don't know how he heard me*, but, smiling he said, "You tell Ruth to get better. Roy and Dale would want her to have a picture." WHEW! mission accomplished.

I came across pictures of the Mars Theatre with all the girls in pigtails. What was that all about? I'm sending along the pictures, and I will talk with you about them, when I see you next.

Love, Janice

SEPTEMBER

Dear Janice,

You asked about the pigtail pictures at the movie theatre. All I can remember is that, if you wore pigtails to the movie, you could get in for a special price. I liked going to the movies. In those days, you could stay and see the movie again if you wanted—no extra cost—just stay!

I remember going to the Laurel and Hardy movies with Grandma Burrows. We liked to go with her because she laughed so much, and we enjoyed watching her enjoy the movie. You know, I still like movies. I probably have the largest collection in the neighborhood, and I love seeing my favorites over again—usually with popcorn!! Someday I suppose they will be on CD ROM or accessed through the Internet at the touch of a button. I guess some of the things we do as adults are extensions of what we did or our parents did when we were children. That reminds me again about how important childhood is and the influences that shape our lives. Ah, childhood—that magical time.

Well, better close for now—see you soon,

Love, Ruth Anne

Notes about your favorite movies, going to the movies, and how this has changed with TV. What about favorite TV shows?

Dear Ruth,

All this talk about the things we did on Main Street makes me think of street kids. Yes, I really was a street kid in La Porte City. Some of the first pictures of me were taken on Main. With Mom and Dad working, we spent much of our time playing on the sidewalk in front of cafe. The Kober girls were street kids, too. Lucky for us, they lived in that apartment on Main, just a few doors down from the Wishmore above their grandfather's insurance office.

Being on Main was an important part of my feeling good about growing up. I especially liked the time we spent skating. How many times do you suppose our skates let go from our feet because they were the kind that clipped to our shoes? I couldn't begin to count the number of skinned knees I'd have in a single summer.

Remember how the four of us, Dotty, Carol, you and I, spent our summer afternoons on Main identifying cars from different states? This was the time when there was a continuous stream of cars through town. Cars coming from the northwest on Highway 218 crossed the bridge, passed directly in front of the Wishmore, and at the hotel corner turned right before continuing southwest directly out of town. Parading up and down Main on our skates, we dashed in and around adults along the way. "You girls are really going fast," Mrs. Kober would say. "Any cars from Ohio today?"

Dotty checked her list, "No, not yet, but some from Illinois."

"Now let's get stationed, so we don't miss any," I commanded and tended to direct the action. "You and Carol skate toward the hotel corner." Dotty and I would take full skate strides and race for the KP corner to catch a glimpse of cars' license plates as they crossed the bridge. I took the first one; Dotty would take the next. If the car didn't have a front plate (many out of state cars only had a rear plate), we would start skating to keep up with the car so as it passed, we could read the rear bumper plate.

"Nope, didn't get it." I would report. Signaling down the way, "Hey, Ruth, Carol, get that one. It's yellow with black; might be from New York!" Carol streaked along the hotel side and then with a quick halt, "Got it. No, it's Ontario!" And, Ruth, as your metal wheels screeched to a quick halt at the hotel corner, and you crouched down getting a bird's-eye-view of the car as it slowed down to make a right hand turn, you would confirm in a declarative voice, "Ontario. Yes, it's ONTARIO!" That was a great find, or for that matter, one from New York, California, New Mexico, or Oregon would have been as well. Cars coming from the south were a bit more difficult to identify because we didn't have anyone on the other side of the street. Nevertheless, I don't believe we missed very many. On any given summer day, we would identify cars from as many as 35 states.

Eventually I could always count on someone saying, "Hey, Janice, your Mom is looking for you." It was always kind of a pain for me. It seemed like everyone knew where we were, and if it wasn't apparent, they would inquire about us when they arrived at the Wishmore.

Upper left–Bill & Bea Ann Ballheim, Ruth, Shirley Sides, Janice, cousins Sharon and Glenda, best friend Bev Sides. Upper right–Janice. Lower left–Claudette & Lynette Nanny. Lower right–cousin Nancy Gae Goon, Janice.

Ruth, I don't know how you felt, but even though we grew up with the Kober kids on Main, it was the Sides family in our neighborhood on Locust that was especially important to me. You were probably too young to remember much. I have written two stories about these times, and I am enclosing them for you. For now, I need to close. I am going to be printing some of Dad's pictures in the darkroom at the Hearst Center next week. I can hardly wait. The darkroom is becoming my time travel room. It is, as if by magic, when the pictures begin to appear as they shimmer in the chemicals and draw me to another of our childhood times.

Until next time, your sis, Janice

BEST FRIENDS PART

Of all the friends we had on Main and around town, I would have to say that I considered Bev my best friend. Even though she was 4 years older than I, we did a lot together. The Sides family lived up the way, across the street, and on the hill. Their family was quite different from ours. There was Bev, the youngest, then Shirley, Thelma, and the four boys, Lloyd, Chuck, Harold, and Warren. All four boys served in the Armed Forces. Pictures of these boys in their uniforms decorated their living room. Bev and I played together there, and sometimes Shirley joined us. I thought their house was huge! The porch ran along two sides of the house and was the place we could pretend to be anything we wanted. In those days, we played cowboys, cowgirls, soldiers, and school teachers.

Many of my dreams were dreamed on the Sides' porch and in their house. In the front parlor, on summer afternoons, Bev and I played paper dolls. We had dolls from all of the armed forces. The faces of the dolls are etched in my mind as if they were real people. I rarely played with Tony, the Air Force guy, because Bev liked him best. I usually had Drew, the sailor. The women wore uniforms, too, the Wacs and Waves. We made houses from an imaginary space by the sofa or in a box. In the next room, we could hear the radio playing the music of the soaps, Young Widow Brown and the Life and Times of Stella Dallas. Many times the aroma of bread Mrs. Sides was baking wafted through the house. My mouth watered, but never once did she offer us any. You know, Ruth, we always had everything we wanted from our kitchen, but then, again, we didn't have a family of 7 children, including 4 growing boys!

With the start of school in the fall, the paper dolls and all activities at the Sides' house ended. One year, after a long winter, I could hardly wait to get to Bev's house to break open the paper doll box. I donned a brand new play suit and sandals that Mom and I had shopped for in Waterloo. Along with a trim haircut and a bigger bow than ever in my hair, I was ready for summer play. Most often Bev and I would see each other around and simply began our play. This year was different. I hadn't seen her around. Anxious for play to begin, I skipped up the street and bounced up the sidewalk stairs. The swing, hanging between the two oaks, seemed lonely. It hung limply with the old tire slightly bobbing around. On the sidewalk, no hopscotch chalk marks yet! "Hmm," I thought, "better get going." I vaulted up the side porch stairs and looked through the screen door. About to knock, the door swung open. "Hi! Hey, Bev, let's ..." I stopped short! Yes, it was Bev.

Who was this person? She wore a big, flared blue and red skirt, with a frilly white blouse. I looked at her eyes—black and blue around them and bright red lips. Her cheeks were pinker than ever. No pigtails; instead, a big swoop of hair up with a gold clasp along the side.

Speaking in a rather aloof way and looking me up and down, she said, "Well, Janice, now what can I do for you?"

"Janice?" I thought. She never calls me "Janice." It's always been "Jannie!" "Well... well-ah, I wondered about... about the... the paper dolls, ... the officers and Wacs, how they must be wanting to see us." My voice was now becoming a bit more assertive. "And the hopscotch, too, I'll get the chalk." Complete silence. We both stood and looked at each other.

Flipping her skirt around and turning her nose up a bit, then with a wave of her hand, she said, "Oh, you mean those old paper dolls? Oh, they went out with the trash. I have no idea when. I'm much too busy to think of such things."

My heart sank. How could she do such a thing! They were so perfect. And, well, now I felt so awkward. I didn't know what to say. "Well ...but ..." I turned around and darted off the porch. The remainder of the day I sat on the edge of our sand box. My tears fell in the sand like droplets of rain, and I scribbled notes in the sand. That summer I spent most of my time with the Main Street kids, even if I was a bit older. The summer passed, but a part of me still yearned for the porch and all the make believe. The swing stood silent and was finally taken down. I wasn't a part of the porch gang anymore. They became high school boys hollering and girls giggling. I experienced a great divide between Bev and me for several years, until I began to wear frilly whites and flared skirts.

Clarinets for Girls, Not Cornets

Ruth, I have probably never told you how I became interested in music. In our neighborhood, during the summer evenings, I could hear the Pearson boy playing his cornet, and maybe the next evening, from the other end of the neighborhood, Lloyd Sides would practice his cornet. I knew that I wanted to play a cornet, too, and I finally convinced Dad that I did! At the time, Al Cole, who had the local shoe repair shop, taught band at school as a side interest. Dad took me to Al Cole's store. Inside the shop, shoe boxes lined the walls. A large workbench on the back was stacked with leather and parts of shoes. The new leather and the shoe polish made a special smell that I liked. Al Cole wore a brown bib leather apron with large pockets. He seemed like an old man to me. "So, you want to play an instrument. Let's see now. Tell me what you hear." With this, he sang a rendition of "Home on the Range" or something of that sort. He pointed to me, indicating he wanted me to sing the next line, sort of a fill-in-the-blank. I must have passed this test because he said, "Ok, now, let's see. Yes, a clarinet. Girls are good at clarinets. I have several."

"Oh," I thought. "It's not the clarinet I want. No, No!" My crying inside almost burst to my outside. One tear did get out, but I quickly wiped it away. Before I knew it, Mr. Cole had wrapped my hands around the long black stick with all the conglomeration of keys, pressing each finger over the keys one at a time. "Whoops, Jannie, your fingers are too small," he exclaimed in a blaming-like manner! "George, look. See how her fingers go through the holes instead of covering them? This won't work. That's a heck of a note!"

Oh, I was so relieved! For once, being small was paying off! Now with all the courage I could muster, meekly, and in a low, fast voice, I looked up directly into Mr. Cole's deep black eyes and bravely said, "I want to play the cornet!"

His eyes widened, throwing his hands up in surprise, "George, so your *little girl* wants to play the cornet?" Crossing his arms, rocking from side to side one foot to the other, shrugging his shoulders, he gave a glance to Dad. Dad made no reply. "Well, I might have… I have only one cornet left. I imagine she could try." Picking up a bright silver cornet, Mr. Cole took the mouthpiece. "Now, this is the way you pucker your lips," he said as he puckered and made a buzzing sound. "Then you do the same with the mouthpiece." He placed the mouthpiece in the horn and helped me place my hands in a correct manner over the three valves.

No need to show me, I thought. I had watched Lloyd practice so many times. Without hesitation I placed the horn to my mouth and blew. Tuu oo. oo…t

"Wow!" Al Cole was taken with great surprise. "Your little girl played a perfect G, a perfect G!" Dad grinned from ear to ear. I was bursting with excitement. I was thrilled. Of course, I could play this cornet!

Dad bought the cornet for $35.00, a silver, used one with a black case lined in green felt and somewhat dirty. To me, however, it was a glittering jewel. I grabbed it tightly and walked proudly out the door. I started to take lessons. I then began to listen to everything on the radio and to play records on the Jukebox at the Wishmore over and over again. This is when I began to fall in love with music for a lifetime.

Dear Jan,

I so enjoyed your letter about the skating and the friends we had on Main Street. You know, being a street kid in those days didn't have the same negative connotation as it would these days. Even though our house and loving home was at 604 Locust Street, our "home" was also on Main Street. We had most of our friends there. The only kids I can remember on Locust were the Sides girls and later Butch and Lydia Larum, who lived next door for only a short time. And, yes, I did play paper dolls with you girls a few times. I can remember having a play grocery store in the Sides' basement stacked with empty food containers.

The other kids were on Main Street—our other home. It was home because we were there a lot but also because those people—the community people—were also a "family" to us. I'm sure they were very aware of our presence, our "growing up" before their eyes. We felt at home on Main Street, were not afraid, and could play at ease. Mom and Dad always knew where we were. We had to ask if we wanted to go out of the block or into our friends' homes. We were free to come and go in and out of the restaurant. If we needed anything, the cafe was there for us. Mom and Dad, Nina, and Grandma Abel were there for us. After the booths had been added to the cafe, there was room on the north wall just inside the door for an ice cream freezer. That was where the fudgecycles, popsicles, and frosticks were kept. We could have one anytime. Our parents never blinked an eye—it was ours to have.

We often played in the backyard of the cafe. There were some grassy areas and some trees there, but the concrete of the front sidewalk was my favorite. That's where the action was! Oh, yes, I remember the roller skating—and the skates. I still have a "skate key" for the old skates that have long gone. We needed a key to tighten the clamp on our shoes or to change the length of the skate. The skates were held on with a leather strap at the ankle and with a clamp on the sides of the toe. We wore the key on a string around our neck so it would be handy.

I can almost hear the screech, scratch, screech of the metal wheels on the concrete as we skated with energy up the street to catch sight of the license plates. The wheels wore thin and collapsed. I wonder how many pairs we wore out? Janice, I don't believe you did, but when I grew up to a young adult, I bought "shoe skates" with fiber wheels and skated at the local wood floor skating arena. It was a portable rink set up in the park—only in the summer. That skating eventually led to ice skating, which I took up as an adult. Cindy and I enjoyed that pleasure together at the Waterloo ice rink.

The license plate search was the best game that we invented. We spent many hot days that turned into cool nights up and down the block on Main Street.

Another game we used to play was throwing a ball over a garage, remember? As we threw a ball over the garage we yelled, "Auntie, Auntie I over." If the person on the other side did not catch the ball, they would yell "pigtail" and then throw the ball back over the garage. If the person did catch it, they said nothing and came running around the garage to tag the other player. I recall spending many evenings in the summer playing this game until dark and the fireflies came out.

I spent many days and hours with the Kober girls. If we weren't skating on the front sidewalk, we were doing something in their apartment or playing in the backyard. We would spend many summer nights in the dark shadows of the backyard trees playing hide and seek. In the summer sun, we enjoyed bikes, flowers, and dolls. Going up the Kober's front apartment steps was an everyday event, and I can still remember how old and worn the steps were. The door opened into a big empty room—sort of like a hallway, but much wider. It had linoleum flooring and was a great place to play with dolls. We often set up card tables and put blankets over them to make tents to play under. Carol and I played classical music in the big room. We pretended we were ballet dancers and spun around with scarves and lace dresses to the Strauss waltzes. Those everyday things became so ingrained in my mind that I will never forget them.

Neighbor and classmate,
Gary Heyden and Ruth
on Locust street.

The Nanny's operated the cleaners on the corner (KP Building). I first became acquainted with Claudette. She welcomed a girlfriend her age because they were new in town. I remember the first time I saw her. She was leaning over tightening her roller skate. It was that moment that I knew that she would be my friend. When she came to Jr. High for the first time, there weren't enough desks in the assembly hall. Miss Fleming said firmly, "Claudette will sit with you, Ruth Anne, until we get another desk." Of course, I was delighted to have "the new girl" sharing a desk with me. Claudette became my best friend through many years of school. It became a regular routine for me to arrive at her door to spend some time with her and Jane, her younger sister. They always had many chores to do, and I either watched or helped. There were even more chores when their baby sister arrived. It was of great interest to me to watch them care for a new baby. I had never been around babies very much. We all enjoyed seeing Lynette grow up to become a sweet young girl. They also had a springer spaniel "Penny" who had several litters of puppies. We had fun playing with the puppies in the backyard of the cleaners. I learned a lot from the Nanny family. They were hard workers, a strong family who also had Grandma living with them.

Nancy Elliott was some younger than I, but we often played together in her backyard or in her room upstairs above the beauty shop. Her mother, Dorothy Kiedle Elliott, was a beautician and seemed always to be busy. The smell of the permanents permeated the whole house. Dorothy was a cheerful person and was always nice to us. Her husband, Russ, was easygoing and a fun guy to be around. He worked for the city light plant (utilities). Our parents would often join them for an after-work-get-together, a well deserved rest after a long and busy day.

I could easily walk in and out of any of these homes and feel just as comfortable as in my own house on Locust Street. To me, it seemed like a big, happy family. Everybody got along and helped each other. The thought of the Main Street folks brings back happy memories of relaxing times with our parents, memories of their laughter drifting out over the backyards of Main Street.

Better close for now — 'til next time, Your sis, Ruth Anne

Notes about childhood friends and neighbors. Activities and games you played.

OCTOBER

Dear Ruth,

1945 was a big year for us, both in our home life and in the world. Let me review the events of that year as I recall them. First, on March 9, a Friday, the folks had a fire. The fire was in a building next to the Wishmore that they had just purchased a week earlier. The folks intended to eventually add a dining room to the cafe. On this fire day, we were in school. Everyone in town heard the fire sirens. From the fifth grade classroom, we could see the smoke coming from the buildings on Main. At first, I was concerned it was our cafe, but soon it was reported it was the place next door.

Normally, when school was out for the day, we would have gone home on our own, but on this day Aunt Nina picked us up and took us to the mayor's office located across the street from the fire. Mom and Dad were scurrying around trying to help the firemen. Everyone was concerned that the fire would spread to other buildings, so the equipment from the cafe had been removed as well as furnishings from other adjoining businesses. The firefighters had equipment up and down the block and were hosing down roofs on all buildings in the block, especially the hotel. Standing across the street, I could feel the heat of the fire on my face and smell the burning wood. Along with all the shouting and chatter as the fire equipment was moved about, I wondered if our town block wouldn't be burned to the ground. I was scared what might happen to our family!

The building the folks had purchased was completely destroyed. The *Progress Review* reported: "Damage estimated to exceed $5000.00 was suffered in the business section that largely destroyed the Haymond Cafe building and ate away the upper part of the L. J. Robertson's law office next door... the fire raged more than two hours before being brought under control, and for a time threatened to engulf the remainder of the block.... A cement fire wall and the wind saved the Wishmore Cafe from damages."

A few days after the fire, I went with Mom and Dad into the destroyed building. The smell of burnt wood remained, and the charred timbers seemed especially tall and threatening as I walked among them. The building had an upstairs apartment the folks had hoped to rent, but they found out the insurance would not cover rebuilding a two level structure. The new building became a one story dining room and was opened in June of 1945.

Main Street was beginning to look very different. New, also, to Main Street that year was the beginning of the city library located in the mayor's office across from the Wishmore. With Mayor Roy Hawkins' leadership, the city council approved a plan to renovate a room. Gale Ballheim, local carpenter, constructed the room with volunteer help from the Lions Club. This made my life very different. Now I didn't spend idle evening time at the counter. If the library was open, Mom and Dad could assume that I was there.

Everything that happened in 1945 was memorable, even to me, a ten year old. When Roosevelt died, everyone huddled next to the radio for announcements. Soon, on VE (victory in Europe) Day, May 8th, everyone was in the street celebrating. On VJ (Victory over Japan) Day, I was in Cedar Rapids with Uncle Bill, Aunt Florence, and Nancy Gae, at a picnic in Beaver Park. Announcement of the Japanese surrender came while we were eating. We gobbled our food down and went downtown to celebrate. It was the biggest parade I had ever seen. People were honking their car horns and waving flags. I was so shocked to see a "Jap" straw man being dragged along behind a car and people cheering! Today, of course, the term "Jap" (Japanese) would never be used, but it was commonly used during WW II.

This is what I remember about 1945. I didn't know it at the time but events of 1945 marked endings, but also new beginnings for a very different life after the war. It was like the curtain was being drawn, on a different looking Main and different times, a Main that we would come to call ours, growing up in the '40s.

TABLES
CAFE
CLUB ROOM
Hiawatha "BEST BIKES BUILT" SOLD EXCLUSIVELY BY Gambles

The picture I am enclosing sets the scene for a typical day on Main after the War. These were booming times. People were always mingling on the street. Look closely and you can see Kober's Real Estate office (the sign mid-center); I can imagine Mr. Kober sitting at his big pigeon hole desk in the window of his insurance business. He always wore a dark suit with a vest. From his watch pocket, a gold chain dangled that set off his silver hair and blues eyes. Next to Kober's Real Estate office, clients would be waiting to see L. J. Robertson, Lawyer. He and Dad worked together to finish the faces of their upper buildings alike after the fire. In the hotel building, Dr. Buser had his office where ailing patients would be packed in a small waiting area. Next door, men were getting a hair cut or shave from Clyde Jenks. Note his barber pole in the picture. On many hot summer afternoons a good place to sit was on Clyde's stone step into his shop. In continual shade, it was always cool. The aroma of hair oil and shaving soap lingered in the summer air. The steady swishing sound of Clyde running his straight edge razor across leather sharpening straps that hung on the side of his barber chair gave a rhythm to the accompanying sounds on Main. At the moment this picture was taken, however, Clyde wasn't doing that. He is the large man in the white shirt standing in the center of the picture.

Apartments located above businesses being very hot in summer, (no air conditioning) brought the occupants to Main for a good share of the day This was true of Jack Betts and his wife, Arlene, standing on the sidewalk beyond the cafe.

As the day progressed, people moved in and out of the Main Street scene. Hank Kruse, town Marshall, had his office in the mayor's office across from the Wishmore and would be seen in and about most of the day. Harold Johnson would make a quick run to the cafe for coffee between customers in his little grocery store. Max Thompson, owner of the Jack and Jill Grocery, made a daily delivery to the Wishmore and would have a daily chat with Dad. At meal times, you could always count on businessmen heading for the Wishmore. Glen Byam from his department store would come first, then his wife. Doc Bailey was always in a hurry; Keith Kline would saunter down the way having spent a morning selling refrigerators and the best in electric stoves. Leo Lewis would dash over when there was a lull in his hardware business. As long as parking places held out on Main, there were large numbers of shoppers—eating at the Wishmore, picking up groceries, stopping for gasoline, or simply taking a break from highway travel.

For sure, Fred and Cora Garrabrant could not be forgotten. They owned the jewelry and fine gift shop in the next block. They were by most called, Mr. and Mrs. Garrabrant, but sometimes with a slip of the tongue, Mr. Garrabrant became Freddy. Mr. Garrabrant wore a suit, immaculately tailored, and in the summertime, a straw hat. Cora, considerably taller than rather round Freddy, wore soft lacy-like dresses, mostly pastels with jewelry. Most often, they didn't appear at the cafe until later in the evening after they closed their shop. They preferred to sit in the dining room rather than in the booth section, as also did Doctor and Mrs. Paige.

Without a doubt, Garrabrants Gift Shop had the most dazzling window displays in town with sparkling rings and bracelets, watches, fine billfolds and tie clasps, fine china and cut glassware. Inside the store was like being in a different world. The street noises were immediately lost to the quiet ticking of clocks mixed with the aroma of fine perfumes. Inside the front door, behind the front window, Mr. Garrabrant often sat wearing a special pair of magnifying glasses. Hovering over tiny clock wheels and cogs, he mended them with great precision. On one side of his desk, fine surgical-like tools lay in neat patterns. Against the back wall there were many tagged watches hanging ready for pick up. Glass cases lined the single aisle of the narrow store.

It was only on special occasions that I went in the store, but I remember one such occasion very well. Dad and I entered the store. Mr. Garrabrant, working on a watch, meticulously laid his tool aside, looked up over his glasses, and in a surprised fashion remarked, "Oh, it's you, George." Getting up, he extended his hand for a shake. "George, good to see you. What can I do for you? Something for the little lady, I imagine." Dad nodded. Mr. Garrabrant, gesturing to a big glass case continued, "Perhaps a piece to add to Faye's candlewick, or silver set?" Hesitating, getting no response from Dad, he continued, "We have new table cloths with matching napkins, or for summer we have specially-designed picnic tableware."

"No, nothing like that today," Dad replied. "Something a bit more personal."

By this time, the sparkle of special gifts in the brightly polished glass cases caught my attention: dolls in fancy costumes, necklaces with all colors of stones in velvet cases, a whole shelf of music boxes! Mrs. Garrabrant followed me. She didn't know I had strict orders not to touch anything! Oh, the doll in the red dress. I had a hard time keeping my fingers off her lacy dress. Intuitively, Mrs. Garrabrant took the doll from the shelf and held it out for me to touch. Next, she turned the key to a small silver box so the music would play and the miniature ballerina would spin in a perfect pirouette. Then I heard Mr. Garrabrant say, "We have just received this limited edition of fine watches." Placing a number of small boxes on the counter, he opened them one by one. The delight on Dad's face was obvious.

"I want to see, too," I exclaimed, running back to the front case!

Dad took a small velvet-covered box and held it on my level, "This is just right, don't you think?"

I peered in. Laying inside, on a soft pink satin lining, was a watch on a pin. One hanging from a bow with pink stones. It was so beautiful! "Oh, yes. Mom will love it." And you know, Ruth, she did! Yes, it had practicality. Mom could hardly wear a wrist watch with her hands in food and water so much, but much beyond that, her face glowed when she received it, and for years thereafter smiled with the memories it endeared. (Shown in picture of Mother, page 59, twice!)

Yes, this is the Main that I am carried back to, whenever I visit La Porte City, Iowa. When my heels click on the brick street, it is the Main Street of the '40s that come alive for me. Ruth, we have talked so much about our town we need to get together and make a map. Surprisingly, last Sunday when the family was here for dinner, I realized there was some confusions about some of the places we were talking about. If you have anything to add, let me know.

Until I see you next, Love Jan.

Our LaPorte City in the '40s

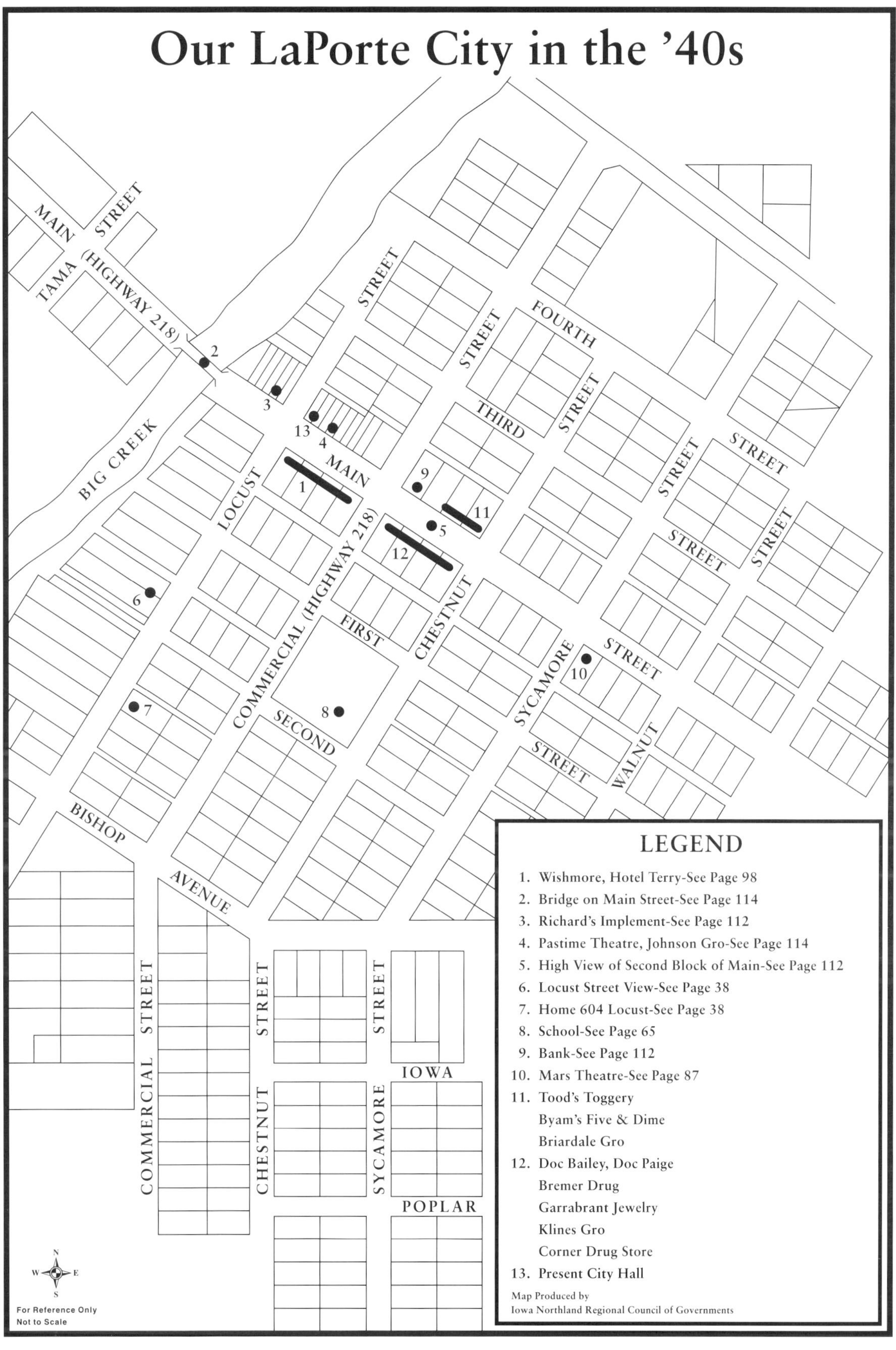

LEGEND

1. Wishmore, Hotel Terry-See Page 98
2. Bridge on Main Street-See Page 114
3. Richard's Implement-See Page 112
4. Pastime Theatre, Johnson Gro-See Page 114
5. High View of Second Block of Main-See Page 112
6. Locust Street View-See Page 38
7. Home 604 Locust-See Page 38
8. School-See Page 65
9. Bank-See Page 112
10. Mars Theatre-See Page 87
11. Tood's Toggery
    Byam's Five & Dime
    Briardale Gro
12. Doc Bailey, Doc Paige
    Bremer Drug
    Garrabrant Jewelry
    Klines Gro
    Corner Drug Store
13. Present City Hall

Map Produced by
Iowa Northland Regional Council of Governments

Memo to: Jan
From: Ruth
Regarding: Main Street Map

It was great to get together to make a little map. It started me thinking about some businesses the i frequented "on down the street." In the second block of Main (same block as Dr. Paige and Dr. Bailey) about half way down, on the same side of the street, Harry Kline had a Meat Market. It had a meat counter that you could see into and choose meats. We would have a list, and the grocer would fill the order. Nowadays, even the little neighborhood grocery stores are self service. Mr. Kline often told me that I could go around the counter and into the back room to see his parrot in a cage. I don't know why he had a pet parrot in the storeroom. I was a little scared of it but wanted to see it. If you've seen the cage in my basement today, well, that's the one! Another treasure from the past.

Across the street from Kline's was the five and dime store or Byam's. I liked going there because the Byam's had a lot of neat things. I was usually buying little candy-filled trinkets or candy dots on a strip. We shopped for school supplies and Christmas gifts at Byam's.

Do you remember the corner drug store? Same side of the street as the Kline Grocery. I don't know about you, but when I was a preteen, I spent a lot of time there with my friends. We would get cherry cokes from the fountain and "mud" desserts made with ice cream, marshmallow cream, and hot fudge. We often bought comic books and movie magazines there. It was a favorite gathering place in town for kids.

Our Main looks a lot different today, but the next time you drive through La Porte City, Jan, look for the remnants of the street we once knew—you'll see some.

Click your heels on the brick and smile,

Ruth Anne

Notes about major world events that impacted your life.
A major war? Major discoveries? What were you doing at the time of these important events? How did these events make a difference to your daily routine?
Can you recall what your mother or dad said about these events?

Two remnants still standing on main Street. Can you find them?

OCTOBER

Dear Ruth,

I've been thinking. The new dining room really did bring new life to the Wishmore, to Main and to the whole community for that matter. The dining room became the place for club parties and celebrations. The expectations from customers were different; literally, there was a "new clientele," as the newer customer put it. The most dramatic contrast to the counter customers were the La Porte City ladies who had luncheon and afternoon parties. I can recall some of the names: Mrs. Anton, Mrs. Goon, Mrs. McGill, and Mrs. Paige. Others, I can't remember, and for the story I am about to tell, perhaps it's just as well.

The ladies would make an appointment with Mother to make the arrangements for their event. For Mother, it was a matter of practicality for fear they might appear at noon or some other busy time. For the customer, the appointment was sometimes a bit more. The memorable feature of this story is that of the two women; the taller one wore a hat with a feather that bobbed when she walked and talked. The two always had parties together. On this occasion, they appeared at the counter announcing, "We have an appointment with Mrs. George Abel." Counter talk stopped—instant silence, a rare sort of thing. A few of the guys switched their chatter to a stare into their coffee cups; others took a quick sip. Still another stretched his neck. Looking up, his eyes caught the bobbing feather, and his head bounced momentarily until he found the familiar face under the hat, his next door neighbor. With a sigh, he said, "Oh, it's you, Tess," breaking the silence. He then quickly turned to continue his counter chatter.

Dad, making a gesture toward the door connecting to the dining room, replied, "Faye will meet you in the dining room." Because the dining room was open only during meal times, Mother generally met with her "appointments" at a back table. Often, I sat nearby. Invariably, these meetings would start, "Now, Mrs. Abel, we'd like a little something *special*. Perhaps you have something—a bit of dessert or a special luncheon salad, something light and scrumptious!" Mother would begin to make suggestions, "Maybe a lemon chiffon, or raspberries will be in season. Perhaps a pie or tart of raspberries with a bit of whipped cream and a little chocolate along the side?" Not hearing any response, she would continue on. "And here is a new something I have been going to try. It's a . . ."

"Oh, splendid! Something new, introduced at OUR party!" and then pausing, "It would be tastie, wouldn't it?" The other interrupting, "Oh, of course, it would, Tess!"

"Let me tell you a little bit about it," Mother would courteously reply and continued on until . . .

"Now, then, we would like to be served before the 12 of us play bridge. You know, we could have this at home, but we want this in YOUR dining room, . . ."

The other chirping in, "You know, I think last time Madge entertained at home, it wasn't even in the *Progress Review!*"

Not acknowledging this remark, the other continued, "Well, but we don't care what the

You are cordially invited to attend
the wedding of
Miss Babs Eleanor Andersen
and
Mr. Borge Jessen
Friday, the sixteenth day of October
Nineteen hundred and fifty-three
at five-thirty o'clock in the afternoon
American Lutheran Church
La Porte City, Iowa
Reception following
at Abel's Cafe

charge is for the room." Then lowering her voice, "but what would the charge be anyway?" They both leaned slightly forward, their heads in a huddle. Now I could only hear jabbering, but the feather was really bob bob bobbing along. Soon, however, with a demonstrative flair, they got up to leave. "Oh, splendid, marvelous! It will be such a scrumptious afternoon," they declared and quickly exited the door and disappeared.

Now, too, I could do something with a flair! I stood up, put my right hand back of my head, my left on my hip, and imitated their animated walk. Tilting my head, and rolling my eyes, I said in rather an affected way, "Now, Mother, dear, so sorry that I don't get to serve this very *special* party, since I will be in *school*."

"Now, Janice." Mother cut me short, but I know she was snickering inside.

The parties I really liked to serve were the regular clubs like BPW (Business and Professional Women) and Lions Club. I especially liked these groups because they were the people we would see every day in their stores or on Main. Yes, the BPW did do things with a flounce and flurry, but they always had good programs, most often speakers or the like. The girls that served them could stay in the dining room for the program.

The Lions Club was loud and roaring, but I really liked this group because, rather than a sit-down-served dinner, each one got his own plate at the serving window. It was truly a community line up. One at a time, each man peered through the window as he grabbed his plate: Roy Hawkins, mayor; Harold Johnson, grocer; Max Thompson, grocer; Bob Estep, Ford Motor; Keith Kullmer, Evergreen Hatchery; Clark, Chevy dealer; Glenn Byam, dime store; Max Taylor, DX station; Leo Lewis, hardware; Harold Gates, barber; Doc Bailey and Doc Paige; Doc Hindman, Chiropractor; Jesse Kober, real estate; Harold D. Matt, school superintendent; many school teachers; most all city councilmen; and often, some of the local ministers.

It was the activity after Lions meetings, however, that I became increasingly curious about. Unlike any other time in the dining room, as soon as all but a few of the guys had left, the blinds on the front window were closed. All the lights were turned out except one over a table in the back of the dining room, and the two doors and serving window connecting the shop side were shut tight! Noticing that a few guys always hung around after the meeting, at first I didn't think much about it. Perhaps they had a special committee meeting for all I knew. Dad must be on a special committee, I thought. But somehow that didn't quite work. Mom and Dad never said anything about it; in fact, their silence and almost secrecy about it made it even more mysterious. Something told me not to ask, but I became so curious, I just had to find out what was going on. So, the very next time, when all this was happening, I opened the dining room door just a wee bit so I could hear. "Remember," I heard my Dad say, "all money off the table."

I opened the door just a bit wider and peeked in. Seven men were sitting around the table. They all held cards; most had a stack of chips nearby. "Match you and call," I heard one say. I paused … They were playing poker! Yow, I shut the door!

No wonder! This is why Mother always seemed a little miffed on Lions night. That night I lost a lot of sleep, imagining what would happen if my Dad and all the guys had to go to jail! Main Street might be closed! I knew the town Marshall made security rounds to all the business places nightly. I had seen him do it so many times as I sat at the counter waiting for Mom and Dad to finish closing up. So I began to watch and notice—same patterns every night, until Lions club night. On these nights, he stayed on the other side of the street. How about that!

Ruth, what about the flaming puddings Mom served? I know it was a big hit with many groups who had parties at Christmas time. Everyone anticipated the serving of the flaming pudding, along with all the other Christmas decorations and candles. Do you have the recipe? Send it, please.

Here's to Roaring Lions and Flaming Puddings!

Janice

Dear Jan,

The times spent at the restaurant were especially important to me because I learned so much from Mom about preparing and serving foods. I have come to enjoy it at home, but, I'm sure, not with the same passion that Mom had. I only entertain occasionally, whereas she was in the business for 40 years!!

I helped serve Sunday dinners in the dining room for a long time. (Seemed like years, but it was probably only the 2 or 3 years before going to college.) About 11:00 a.m. we turned on the lights, unlocked the door, and opened the venetian blinds. That was the signal that all was ready for the Sunday dinners. Mom had been working, however, since early morning. Aunt Nina and Grandma Abel were there with her, probably before the sun came up, making pies first, then the main course, choices of oven fried chicken, ham, and Swiss steak. The potatoes were cooking, almost ready to mash, and the vegetables were heated. The jello salads had been made the night before.

I arrived at the Wishmore about 10:00. "It's just me," I yelled as I walked in the front door. I didn't want Mom to drop her work thinking that I was a customer. "Hi, Honey, all ready for work? You can start in the dining room."

Starting in the dining room meant moving the tables around to their proper places after the Saturday night cleanup, filling the salt, pepper and sugar, peeling apart the paper doilie placemats, and setting each place with a cloth napkin, silver, and coffee cup. I filled a tray of water glasses, ready to serve. "You can get some fresh flowers in the yard," she said. "I saw some new blossoms this morning when I came in the back."

Mom thought of everything, and the place was ready for action. I grabbed my frilly apron and was ready when the lights went on at 11:00. The regular Sunday customers bustled in at the same time every week, and they sat at the same tables every Sunday. I could almost guess what they were going to order. They came dressed in their "Sunday Go-to-Meetin'" clothes: hats and gloves, suits and ties. I prepared the salads, grabbed the rolls and butter, and served them directly from the kitchen. Mom put up the main course and the desserts through the serving window. "Be sure to refill the coffee," she always reminded me. "Watch your customers for anything they need." The correct service and service with a smile were important to Mom. Everything went very smoothly—even when it was very busy. She had a system, and the system worked well. Many Sundays I worked the dining room alone, and if it filled to 40, it was a very busy place. I learned to prioritize very quickly so that the customers were comfortable and happy. We wanted them to return next Sunday!

I also served the Saturday night card parties. This was a large group of people who enjoyed playing cards until late—11:00 or 12:00—and then wanted lunch served. After the regular Saturday evening business and the cafe was cleaned and ready for Sunday, I would go home to rest a while. As I went out the door, Mom would say, "I'll call you about 10:30."

"O.k.," I responded. "I'll try to be awake." I would walk quickly home in the cool night air, listening to the crickets, the highway traffic, and the neighborhood dogs barking.

By this time we had TV—black and white, of course—and I sat down to watch whatever Grandma was watching—usually professional wrestling. After the news on Saturday night, we watched "The Web," a thrilling, sometimes scary mystery. I sat entranced by the story and jumped when the phone rang 2 rings. "Are you awake, Honey?" Mom said. "We're just about ready. The cards are almost done."

"I'll be there in a few minutes." I switched off the TV; Grandma was asleep in the chair. I gave the dog a pat and started for Main Street. The evening had turned to a silent, bone-chilling night, with few sounds except for the crickets. I'd start walking on the sidewalk, missing the familiar bumps in the concrete. The tree shadows and the slightly rustling leaves hurried my feet until I was running. I often thought someone was behind me, but I was too frightened to look back. I was out of breath by the time I came to Main Street and rounded the corner into the safety of the streetlights. Bursting in the door, I'd yell, "I'm here," wide-eyed with a great sigh of relief. Even today I recall the bone-chilling breathlessness whenever I step into a cool summer evening filled with chirping crickets and rustling shadows.

The familiar aroma of the hamburgers mixed with the muffled laughter from the dining room, smoke creeping into the kitchen, and food prepared and waiting all calmed my pounding heart. I grabbed my cotton bib apron and set about preparing the buns and the chips. The hot coffee was brewing and smelled of home. All this, the makings of another fun party in the dining room. I liked serving the card people. They were jovial, had interesting things to talk about, and always gave good tips to the servers. As I entered the dining room, I heard, "Hi, Ruth Anne." Smiles from all around came from many couples who were family friends. They watched with disbelief as I carried out my duties with adult-like skill. Their children were home in bed! "Here's a little extra for your late night work." Change clinking into my apron pocket improved the service with more coffee and a twinkle in my eye.

I distinctly remember Mr. and Mrs. Simmons, an unlikely couple. She, in her plain cotton dress, porcelain white skin, and Marcelled hairdo, looked as if she came directly from the flapper era. She was always smiling, looking as if she would not speak a bad word even if she had a mouth full of them. Mr. Simmons wore tight suspenders around his pot belly. He was a red-faced, gruff-looking man, who smoked a cigar and studied his cards with great intent. On one occasion, we had served the pie with a paper doily under each piece. When his empty plate was removed, his little wife, who was his complete opposite said, "Why, Roy, did you eat the paper doily, too?" His already red face became flushed right up to the top of his bald head. He was reminded and teased about cleaning up his plate at every card party after that.

Yes, I was a young girl doing adult tasks in the dining room. Now, you put that young girl in the middle of an Army convoy and you've got teenage excitement!

Every once in a while and always in the summer, Mom would get a phone call from the U.S. Army saying that the summer camp convoy would be coming through La Porte City and wanted lunch. Mom always said, "Yes, Sir. We'd be glad to serve you fellas. What time will you arrive? We can make available these choices of sandwiches." Mom offered the famous Wishmores, tenderloins, and steak sandwiches, French fries, coleslaw, and, of course, pie and ice cream. "Well, George, we'll have to make extra tenderloins, get extra buns, and get the potatoes cut. I'll make the pies on Friday afternoon so we'll have plenty on Saturday by 11:00. Will you call Mr. Potter and ask to have 2 more 5 gallon cartons of vanilla ice cream delivered on Friday. I'll have Nina start on the cabbage on Thursday." My part was easy. I had set the table so many times. No cloth napkins for these guys. The basic place setting and condiments all stood at attention in repetitive order on the shiny black tables. The plans made, the wheels turning—excitement was rumbling just as the wheels of the convoy were rumbling down Highway 218.

The most important preparation for me was applying just the right amount of lipstick and perfume and finding just the right skirt and blouse to wear! I was probably 13, but I looked much younger and wanted to look much older! I grabbed my white cotton apron with the cute ruffles and was ready for the excitement. The anticipation of the event, however, was better than the real thing. We worked so hard and so fast that I nearly forgot to enjoy the fun of the handsome guys in uniform. I do remember some beckoning glances, and I enjoyed the dashing smiles and the flirting winks as I served the sandwiches and poured yet another cup of coffee. In no time, the guys were finished eating and out the door. The final and everlasting reward of the day was knowing that I liked the work, the people, and the clinking tips in my apron pocket.

When we were little tykes, Jan, do you recall the 40th anniversary celebration we had for our Grandpa and Grandma Burrow in the dining room? The surprise was planned by our Aunt Frances and Uncle Glen. The five of us (grandchildren) played parts in a mock wedding. Costumes were delightfully improvised. I laughed at your slicked back hair, Janice, to make you look like a groom. Sharon was the bride. Glenda was the preacher. I was the flower girl, and Marilyn carried a large "hog-ring" on a satin pillow. The ring was polished to a bright luster, and it all certainly brought out the delight in our grandparents eyes. When the wedding march began, everyone was smiling and singing, "Here Comes the Bride."

Another bridal occasion I especially remember was that of Babs and Borge Jesson. They were new to La Porte City and to the country. They had met in December of 1950 while sailing to Copenhagen on the Swedish ship *Stockholm*. After visiting family in Denmark, they returned to the United States and started a new life together. They were married at the American Lutheran Church in La Porte City. There were few guests in the church, as it was not the Danish tradition to invite friends, but just family members. Babs and Borge's parents were in Denmark (celebrating there). Babs had one family member, Aunt Hildegard Bunde from California, in attendance at the wedding.

They asked Mom to serve the reception. It was 1953. Mother was delighted to serve the reception. For supper, Swiss steak was served, and of course, for dessert, a wedding cake. She used her candlewick crystal dishes to add a special sparkle to the event. Babs and Borge provided a "wreath-cake" (Kranskage), an original Danish tradition. It was decorated with Danish flags and crackers (the little paper roll containing candy etc. that explodes when the ends are pulled). "Congratulations and Til Lykke! (happiness)."

Mock wedding

Say the word "party," Jan, and I'm all ears. My eyes get a special glitter and my mind races to the planning. This must have started early in my restaurant work, as I acquired Mom's enthusiasm for all the preparations. When I was 15 years old, I wanted a party of my own, and Mom was willing to let me arrange the affair for my birthday and use the dining room!

For this special party, I wanted plenty of activity and good foods. The dining room was decorated and plans made for a square dance caller to come for part of the evening. I invited my friends days ahead of time, and we were all talking of the fun to be had as we met at school or over Cokes at the drugstore. The cold, December night finally arrived, and my friends burst into the dining room at the designated hour. They quickly attacked the candy dishes and the soft drinks. The music was turned up, and the square dancers began clapping and stomping to the beat. "Do-Si-Do" and "allemande left" were heard among the sounds of laughter. The tall fellows swung the girls round as the skirts whirled in every corner of the room—the room where just this afternoon quiet games of bridge were played at the shiny black tables. Worn out after a full evening of dance, we collapsed on the floor, leaning against the wall near the serving window. The smell of the hamburgers revived us, and we were soon devouring the food that Mom had prepared, with a special amount of love stirred in for a teenage moment to be remembered a lifetime. Just one of those moments Mom made special for us.

Well, Jan, I guess I must stop rambling. I have a backyard party to plan and a family dinner to serve this weekend. What are your next party plans?

Happy days, Ruth Anne

P.S. I have enclosed some recipes that I found in Mom's cafe cookbook including the one for "flaming pudding." I can still hear the "ohs" and "ahs" and see the brightened faces as this dessert was served for the crowning touch to a special holiday evening. Hope you enjoy using them for your next special occasion.

CELEBRATE!

Dear Jan,

Just a note to tell you that I was thinking about all the people that came to the cafe for one occasion or another. Remembering their shoes clicking on the bricks of the street started me thinking about the many events crossing those bricks.

In a way, our parents participated in everyone's celebrations. Some of America's favorite pastimes are going out to eat—or having a family picnic—a family reunion—a class reunion.

The town celebrations were always a high point in our parents' business. They planned everything around special events: town celebrations, sports, school activities, holiday parties, and the like.

Today La Porte City has the "Festival of Trails"—a three-day event in June. Included are some of the same events from the Jiggs Day era: the parade, the booths, the carnival. Added for nostalgia's sake is a classic car cruise and car show. This often brings back some of the old cars that were new in the Jiggs Day parades!! Let's go together next June, Jan.

I have to run—I'm off to hear my granddaughter sing for the first time in church. I'm sure she'll wave at us from the front of the church, and we'll smile and wave and share this special event with her.

Take time to celebrate something today—and remember all those wonderful times we've spent anticipating the next event.

Happy days,

Ruth Anne

P. S. I have enclosed some photos that I found of the Jiggs Day celebrations.

What are important celebrations for you?
Holidays, special events, or special years in your life? What about special moments?
Talk to your family and friends about them.

View of second block Main. See map, page 101.

Bank building. Can you find Bev Sides and Janice? See map, page 101.

Richard's Implement. See map, page 101.

Dear Ruth,

Yes, Ruth, the years following World War II were boomer years, and our parents were an important part of that in La Porte City. Celebrations and activities on Main went late into the night. I recall many nights the folks would close after everyone else on Main had gone home. The routine was that Dad would go out the back door for the car, and Mom and I would lock up and leave through the front door. On hot summer nights, Dad wouldn't go directly home. He would drive down Main to the six corners and then home via Bishop. Except for the wheels clicking on the brick pavement, the street was silent. The warm breeze stirred the smell of hamburger and fries left in our clothes. We never said it to one another, but I think we all felt like overseers closing down Main for the night. Even though we were tired, we sat high in our seats, knowing that all was well and that we had helped to make it that way.

As with many stories, the prosperous years on Main didn't last. The highway was rerouted and no longer passed the cafe. The early '50s brought TV sets into the home and main streets became suddenly and dramatically silent. People didn't come to Main to socialize, only to run errands and back home again for the next TV highlight. The wind was now the only thing that rattled the screen doors. The smell on Main was of dust, not popcorn. The lights from the Wishmore shown alone in the night. Sitting at the counter looking out the window to a dark silent street, I often felt as though we were in a time warp, lost from the world. Some nights across the way one might see the staggering town drunk. Alone, now, not lost in a crowd. Hours at the cafe became shorter. Dad relied more on his television repair for income. Mother continued to enjoy party business, but profit margins were slim on this local business.

I have often wondered how the hardship of the waning business did really affect Mom and Dad. You probably heard them as I did, talk about changing menus, prices, and hours, but becoming caught up in my own teenage world, I was on the periphery of all this. They faced both changes in business and the fact that their two daughters were soon to graduate from high school. I am sure we never really understood the real sacrifice the folks made to help us attend college.

Ruth, it has been a great venture for me, writing these letters, and especially seeing all the stories in our pictures. Now we need to finalize our pages so that all the grandchildren and others interested may enjoy them. When I see you next, let's close the pages on this journey. Many Happy Days.

Your Sister, Janice

Pastime Theatre, Johnson Grocer. See map, page 101.

Bridge on Main. See map, page 101.

Dear Jan,

This has been an interesting year. It's been a wonderful adventure. Seems like we strolled down the streets of La Porte City every day again. We have been very lucky recipients of many mementos of our childhood. The photos have been a wonderful reminder of times gone by. Everyone should take pictures and carry their camera with them at all times. Seems like the town notables should take regular chronological photos of their town, so pictorial records are kept, not just in the memories of folks like us.

There were many things in La Porte City that we don't have in photos but which live on in our memories only. For instance, do you remember the horse drawn milk delivery? I was fascinated by the horse knowing the route and stopping at regular intervals before completing the round for the day. Do you remember the inside of the old grade school? I loved the floor plan with the large central hall with rooms surrounding in a circle, long coat closets between. The floors were always shiny with varnish and polish, and they were squeaky.

The changes in business in town have been constant and dramatic. Today, the drug stores do not exist; there are now video stores and quick shops. Kramers Sausage Company is in the corner store where Dad started his popcorn stand on the street. There are plenty of beauty shops and banks. Just one grocery store compared to the many that used to be on Main. There are antique shops and country gift and craft shops. Just a few restaurants, none can yet claim to be in business for 40 years as was our parents' cafe.

We can still walk down the streets of La Porte City together looking this way and that. Our heels can still click on the brick street, and we can still see remnants of the past. The mayor's office and city hall still proudly shows its brick face. There are corner stones and whole buildings that still exist from the Wishmore era. There are many that have new fronts and many that are gone. As you look toward lots 207 and 209 Main you will not see the cafe. The old part of the cafe was torn down, the restaurant equipment and furnishings long gone. In its place now stands an empty lot behind a wrought iron gate—a little spot of quietness on Main. Next door is the building that was the dining room. When I walk by now, I look closely at the original door and the windows, the sidewalk in front— remembering again those days and times.

Janice, I want to thank you for the fun we've had reminiscing. Not only have we relived some precious moments, but we have acquired a better understanding of each other. I have learned how important you were to me as I was growing up and how important you are to me now. I may not have become the person that I did without your company, your encouragement, and your advice as we shared a journey together. You are my only close link to a life that is mostly buried but which we have brought to life again on these pages.

Wishes to you,

Ruth Anne

We both graduated from La Porte City High School in the '50s. Following high school, we both attended colleges and became teachers, Janice in music, Ruth Anne in elementary education.

Our parents continued to enjoy the cafe business until they sold the Wishmore and retired in 1970. The cafe changed ownership several times through the '70s and eventually was closed. Mother and Dad continued to live at 604 Locust and to enjoy their retirement with family and friends.

They are both gone now. Dad died in 1978 and Mother in 1994. Our lives have been varied, filled with good times and life's special moments. Part of ourselves will always be in La Porte City, but we look forward to different times, times our parents could never imagine, but dreams that started with them. In our lives now, no matter how passionately we are pursuing a future, no matter how hectic the days, with the first songs of the summer locust we are beckoned back to another place in time—a place where once again we find ourselves sitting around the dinette table in our childhood home, learning and laughing and falling in love with the world all over again.

We hope you have enjoyed the journey with us through the early years of our lives. Our "Wishmore" for you is a reflective journey of your own into the corners of your past.

From our lives to yours, best wishes.

Ruth Anne and Janice Abel

Time waits for no one
See that you use it well
God has placed for you upon this earth
A wondrous flowing well

There flows sweet mysteries
For you to search of every kind
Love full enough and deep enough
For everyone to find.

Little things of nature
Abound in open fields
You could search a lifetime long
And not find all it yields.

You could look forever at the beauty
And giant wonders of the world
See all the relics of the past
Discover the new things glittering and pearled

There are so many pleasures
Of laughter, love and fun.
How do some overlook them
As through life so carelessly they run?

So catch a bucket of all the good things.
There are some you're bound to miss.
As these splash by just touch them gently,
As a rose the soft rain remembers to kiss.

For time waits for no one
There's so many good things to do
There is no time for bad things
God guarantees you'll find this true.

SPRING 1977

Review the notes you have made to begin your journey. What family stories do you have? What others can you think of? Can you fill in any more details? Who said what? Share your stories, objects, and pictures with other family members. Most of all, continue to remember and write. If you need further guidance in writing and recording your life we have listed some resources that may be helpful to you. We found several of these helpful in different ways. Take it one step at a time and enjoy!

A list of things I want to do next...

RESOURCES: WRITING YOUR LIFE STORY

Having written our book, we offer these guidelines.

1. Start now! The younger the better — you are making memories now!

2. Take pictures and write about routine activities in your life; going to work, daily home routines, activities you have done for years. You are not as likely to overlook special occasions like birthdays, holidays.

3. Let your imaginations go! Use media that will motivate all family members: computers, Internet resources, library, camera, video, etc.

4. Have family times to talk about family events routine and special. Are you spread across the miles? Write. Telephone. How about a newsletter? I have received annual Christmas letters that outline a typical day in a family's life as well as ones that tell of the year's family activities and events.

5. Don't "get set" too long. Jump in and just do it!

Here are some book resources we believe can be helpful.

ALBERT, SUSAN WITTIG. *Writing From Life: Telling Your Soul's Story*, Putnam Publishing Group, January 1997. Written for women. Recognize your natural storytelling talents. Provides exercises and examples to inspire writers. Provides framework for writing chapter by chapter about various aspects of your life. Specific suggestions of how family history can be recorded and how to keep the task manageable and fun.

DANIEL, LOIS. *How to Write Your Own Life Story: The Classic Guide for the Non-Professional Writer*, Chicago Review Press, 1997. Describes the process of writing your life. Excellent examples.

GOLDBERG, NATALIE. *Writing Down the Bones*, Boston, Shambhala, 1986. Get the creative juices flowing—good exercises.

GREEN, BOB, D. G. FULFORD. *To Our Children's Children: Preserving Family Histories for Generations to Come*, Doubleday, March 1993. 211 pages. Step-by-step guide to create personal histories from memories of older people. Straightforward questions to inspire memories.

JOYCE, ROBERT D. *Memory Bank Notebook*, Hawthorne House (1509 S. Raitt St., Santa Anna, CA 92704), 1994. A fill-in-the-blanks book. Well done—complete.

KEMPTHORNE, CHARLEY. *For All Time*, Portsmouth, NH: Boynton/Cook Publishers, 1996. Good guide to have as you develop your life story. Especially good in helping you write narratives, scenes from your life!

Lifestory, an interactive monthly newsletter published by Kempthorne and his staff who give you on-going encouragement and writing tips. We used this resource and found it fun and relaxing. It is published by LifeStory Institute, 3591 Letter Rock Road, Manhattan, Kansas 66502.

MERCIER, LAURIE; BUCKENDORF, MADELINE. "Using Oral History in Community History Projects." (Pamphlet Service, Volume 4), 1992. Oral History Association.

NEUBAUER, JOAN R. *From Memories to Manuscript: The Five-Step Method of Writing Your Life Story*, Salt Lake City: Ancestry, 1994. In 40 pages provides suggestions to gather information, organize, write, edit and publish your life story. Concise with good prompts to jog your memory and help you develop your story.

SPENCE, LINDA. *Legacy: A Step by Step Guide to Writing Personal History*, Ohio University Press, 1997. Uses a series of questions about each phase of human life.

THOMAS, FRANK P. *How to Write the Story of Your Life*, Writer's Digest Book, 1984. To get you started, uses many points of departure and pages of questions.

ENTREESS

WISHMORE SANDWICH

Drive In Burgers (this is our own version of the "Wishmore" sandwich—good with or without the catsup)

>   3 pounds ground beef
>   ½ cup chopped onion
>   1 cup water
>   1½ cups catsup
>   4 tablespoons paprika
>   2 tablespoons chili powder
>   1½ teaspoons salt
>   1½ teaspoons pepper
>   1 tablespoon worchestershire sauce.

Brown ground beef with onion. Add remaining ingredients and simmer 10 minutes. Serve on hamburger buns.

CRANBERRY AND APPLE SALAD

(this recipe came from Eva Newton for one of her card parties)

> *Combine:*
>   2 cups chopped raw cranberries
>   3 cups small marshmallows
>   ¾ cup sugar

Chill overnight.

> *Add:*
>   2 cups chopped red apples
>   ½ cups fresh grapes
>   ½ cup nut meats
>   ¼ teaspoon salt
>   Fold in:
>   1 cup whipped cream
>   ¼ cup salad dressing (mayonnaise)

Chill or freeze.

APRICOT CHICKEN

>   1 frying chicken (cut up)
>   1 – 12 ounce jar apricot preserves
>   1 – 8 ounce bottle Russian dressing
>   1 envelope onion soup

Mix apricots, Russian dressing, and onion soup mix. Put the chicken in shallow baking dish. Pour apricot mixture over chicken.Cover with foil and bake 350 degrees for 45 minutes or until chicken is tender.

HOT CHICKEN SALAD

>   4 cups cut up cooked chicken
>   2 tablespoons lemon juice
>   ¾ cup mayonnaise
>   1 teaspoon salt
>   2 cups chopped celery
>   4 hard cooked eggs, sliced
>   ¾ cup cream of chicken soup, undiluted
>   1 teaspoon minced onion
>   1 tablespoon pimento chopped
>   1 cup shredded cheese
>   ½ cup toasted slivered almonds
>   1 – 3 ounce can chow mein noodles

Combine all ingredients except cheese, noodles and almonds. Pour into 9 by 12 pan.Top with last three ingredients. Refrigerate covered overnight. Bake at 350 degrees for 30–35 minutes or until lightly browned and bubbly.

PIES, A CAKE, A COOKY AND A TREAT

LEMON CHIFFON PIE (MOM'S VERY OWN RECIPE)

Mix and set aside:
   1 pkg. unflavored gelatin
   ¼ cup cold water

*Combine, cook, stirring constantly
until mixture coats a spoon:*
   4 egg yolks (use large eggs)
   ½ teaspoon salt
   ½ cup sugar
   ½ cup lemon juice
   1 teaspoon grated lemon rind

Remove from heat and mix the softened gelatin. Mix well, cool until it starts to jell. In the meantime, beat 4 egg whites (room temp.) into a stiff meringue, adding ½ cup sugar gradually. Fold the meringue into the cooled lemon mixture and place in baked shell. (The secret to a high pie is in the beating of the meringue and careful folding into cooled lemon mixture.) It takes a good strong mixer.

APPLE CREAM PIE

Preheat oven to 350 degrees.
Slice apples into prepared unbaked pie crust. Fill crust to desired level.

Mix together:
   ⅓ cup flour
   1 cup sugar
   cinnamon to taste
   dash of salt

Add cream (or ½ pint sour cream) to flour mixture and pour over apples.

Bake 1 hour at 350 degrees until lightly browned.

CHOCOLATE PIE (OR ANY FLAVOR CREAM PIE FILLING)

   1 cup sugar
   ⅓ cup flour
   1 tablespoon (rounded) corn starch
   dash of salt
   3 tablespoon cocoa (coconut, banana, vanilla etc.)
   2 ½ cups milk

Heat 2 cups milk. Add ½ cup cold milk to dry mixture.

Slowly pour into hot milk. Cook to boiling, stirring constantly.

Add:
   1 teaspoon vanilla
   1 tablespoon butter

Cool slightly before pouring into baked pie shell. To prevent crust from soaking up the hot pudding, spread a thin layer of the pudding onto pie shell and let cool before adding the rest of the pudding.

Serve cooled with whipped topping.

FRESH STRAWBERRY OR RASPBERRY PIE

   1 quart fresh fruit
   1 cup water
   1 cup sugar
   2 heaping tablespoons corn starch
      (dissolve in a little cold water)
   dash of salt
   red food coloring as desired
   1 teaspoon vanilla
   1 tablespoon butter
   1 baked 9 inch pie shell

Boil together water, sugar, corn starch. Cook stirring constantly until thick. Remove from heat, add butter, vanilla and coloring. With the back of a tablespoon, put a thin coat of mixture on baked pie crust. (This will help prevent fruit from soaking into the crust.) Alternate prepared fruit with filling ending with the filling and covering fruit. Refrigerate. Serve with whipped topping. Best if served within 3 to 4 hours.

RASPBERRY CHIFFON PIE
>   1 (10 oz.) package frozen red raspberries,
>   thawed, drained
>   1 (3 oz.) package raspberry jello
>   2 tablespoon lemon juice
>   3 egg whites
>   ¼ cup sugar
>   ½ cup whipping cream
>   1 baked pie crust

Dissolve the raspberry jello in ⅔ cup hot water. Using the raspberry juice and lemon juice, make ¾ cup liquid to add to dissolved jello. Chill until slightly thickened. Beat the egg whites. Gradually add ¼ cup sugar. Beat ½ cup whipped cream. When jello is slightly thickened, fold in whipping cream and then the stiffly beaten egg whites. Add the drained raspberries last. Pour into baked pie crust. May be served with whipped topping. Best if served within 3 – 4 hours.

PIE DOUGH (ONE-CRUST PIE)
>   1 ½ cups flour
>   sprinkle with salt
>   ½ cup Crisco (cut into flour)

Gradually add approx. ¼ cup cold water. Stir until dough cleans the sides of the bowl. Roll on slightly floured surface. Arrange in pie pan. For baked crust: prick with fork and bake for 10 – 12 minutes at 450 degrees. For filled crust: bake according to pie filling recipe.

DATE CAKE
(used for the flaming pudding for Christmas) serves 6

Butter and flour 9 x 9 inch pan.
Preheat oven to 350 degrees.

Mix and let set:
>   1 cup dates (cut in pieces)
>   1 teaspoon soda
>   1 cup boiling water

Mix together:
>   ½ cup shortening (margarine)
>   1 cup sugar
>   ½ cup chopped nuts
>   1 ⅔ cup flour
>   1 egg
>   ¼ teaspoon salt

Add to date mixture. Pour into pan. (Double for 12 and bake in 9 x 13 pan) Bake for 30 – 45 mins. Toothpick test.

To serve: Add warm lemon sauce. For a festive touch, dip a lump of sugar in lemon extract and flame.

LEMON SAUCE: (MAKES 1½ CUPS)
>   ½ cup sugar
>   1 tablespoon cornstarch plus few teasp.
>   dash salt
>   1 cup water
>   2 tablespoons butter or margarine
>   1 ½ tablespoon lemon juice (add a little lemon
>   extract or flavoring)

Mix sugar, cornstarch and salt. Gradually stir in water. Cook over low heat, stirring constantly, until thick and clear. Add butter and lemon juice, blend thoroughly.

MERINGUE SHELLS
(Makes 18–24 shells to be served containing ice cream, fruit, or lemon, caramel, or chocolate fillings.)

Beat 6 egg whites (¾ cup) and ⅛ teaspoon salt on high speed until stiff enough to hold shape.

Add 2 cups sugar, 2 tablespoons at a time, beat on low speed about 2minutes after each addition. (Will take about 30 minutes).

Add 1 teaspoon vanilla and 1 teaspoon vinegar to meringue, beat at high speed 10 minutes longer. Shape heaping spoonfuls into individual shells with back of teaspoon onto a buttered baking sheet.Bake at 275 degrees for 45 minutes. Reduce heat to 250 degrees and bake 15 minutes longer until creamy white and firm. Cool on racks. Store in covered container until needed.

LEMON CREAM FILLING (FOR MERINGUE SHELLS)
Beat 4 egg yolks slightly in top of double boiler.

Add:
    ½ cup sugar
    1 tablespoon grated lemon rind
    ¼ cup lemon juice
    ⅛ teaspoon salt

Cook over boiling water, stirring, 8–10 minutes until thick. Cool covered. Whip 1 cup cream until stiff; fold into lemon mixture.Spoon into meringue shells and refrigerate 12–24 hours. Serve with whipped cream and flaked coconut or fresh fruit.

THUMBPRINT COOKIES
    Mix together:
        ¼ cup soft margarine
        ¼ cup soft butter
        ¼ cup packed brown sugar
        1 egg yolk
        ½ teaspoon vanilla

    Sift together:
        1 cup flour
        ¼ teaspoon salt

Add to sugar mixture and mix well. Roll into balls the size of a small walnut. Beat lightly with a fork: 1 egg white. Dip balls into egg white and roll in ¾ cup chopped nuts (pecans) and / or coconut.

Place about 1 inch apart on greased baking sheet. Bake 5 minutes at 350 degrees. Remove from oven. Immediately press thumb gently into top of each cookie. Return to the oven and continue baking for about 5–8 minutes. Cool slightly. Fill each thumbprint with confectioner sugar icing and top with M & M peanut candy. Cool.

ICING:
    1 cup sifted powdered sugar
    ¼ teaspoon vanilla
    milk (add just a little at a time)

Stir together sugar, vanilla and enough milk to make consistency for filling thumbprints.

CARAMEL POPCORN
Prepare 4 quarts of popped corn. Set aside.
    1 pound brown sugar
    1 cup white Karo syrup
    ½ pound butter
    1 teaspoon cream of tartar

Cook to a boil and continue to cook for 5 more minutes. Add 1 teaspoon baking soda. (This will puff up quickly.) Pour over the 4 quarts of popped corn. You may wish to add peanuts to the corn. Stir until coated. Bake at 250 degrees for 1 hour. Stir occasionally while baking and then pour out onto a cool large surface. Stir while cooling to prevent corn from cooling in one big piece.

Special thanks to Bob and Doris Wagner publishers and Diane Roberts, Editor of *The Progress Review*, for the many times we researched their archives, for assistance in copying of materials and for permission to use this material in our book. Thanks to Kevin Blanshan and Jennifer Kragt from Iowa Northland Regional Council of Governments (INRCOG) for preparing the map and for permission to use the map. Thanks to Walden Photo for various services during the development of the collages.

Thanks to all those who provided suggestions and guidance along the way to complete this book. Special thanks to readers, Loren Horton, Phyllis Carlin, Ron Crooks. A very special thanks to Sherry Nuss for her meticulous copy editing through several editions. We feel fortunate to have Philip Fass design this book and also appreciate his efforts in coordinating between design and the printing process.

Thanks to all friends in La Porte City who were willing to share their stories and help us recreate life on Main during the '40s! Events are true and/or typical of the times. Some names of Wishmore customers, we could not remember or identify therefore we used fictitious names. In all cases our story was told with intent to honor and celebrate the lives of many who enriched our childhood in La Porte City, Iowa.

Photo collages were designed by Janice and Ruth Anne using George's photographs.

Photographs are by George Abel with the following exceptions: Mock Wedding (page 110), and Borge Jesson Wedding (page 105); Christmas Card-by Cliff Burr (page 42); Various photos of George and Faye in their earlier years with parents (pages 12, 14, 17); center picture of sisters collage-photographer unknown (page 26). Four generation picture-Emma, Olive, Faye and Janice (page 13).

Additional photographs and movie film of La Porte City 1930-1970 by George Abel are available upon request.

Copies of this book are available in a variety of books stores and directly from the publisher.

Ruth Anne attended Iowa State Teachers College and began teaching elementary school at the age of 19! Continuing to teach as she was raising a family, she completed a B.A. in education at the University of Northern Iowa and later an M.S. degree from Iowa State University. She has taught kindergarten in her hometown of La Porte City for 31 years.

Janice completed a Bachelor's and Master's degree in music education at Drake University. After teaching instrumental music for five years, she completed a Doctorate at Indiana University. She spent a major portion of her professional life at the University of Northern Iowa. She is now an interviewer-writer and amateur photographer.

The text of this book is set in ten point Sabon with 14 point leading; the captions in eight point Sabon and ten point Sabon Italic. This book was printed on seventy pound Fortune Matte by Thomson-Shore of Dexter, Michigan. This printer also did the Smyth sewn binding.